" Astronomy compels the soul
to look upward, and leads us
from this world to another. **"**

-Plato

THEY CHANGED THE WORLD

COPERNICUS · BRUNO · GALILEO

Written by
RIK HOSKIN

Illustrated by
NARESH KUMAR

Colored by
PRADEEP SHERAWAT

Edited by
SOURAV DUTTA & SHREYA MUKHERJEE

Designed by
VIJAY SHARMA

Cover art by
NARESH KUMAR & PRADEEP SHERAWAT

CAMPFIRE®

www.campfire.co.in

Mission Statement

To entertain and educate young minds by creating unique illustrated books
that recount stories of human values, arouse curiosity in the world around us,
and inspire with tales of great deeds of unforgettable people.

Published by Kalyani Navyug Media Pvt Ltd
101 C, Shiv House, Hari Nagar Ashram,
New Delhi 110014, India

ISBN: 978-93-81182-96-3

Printed in India

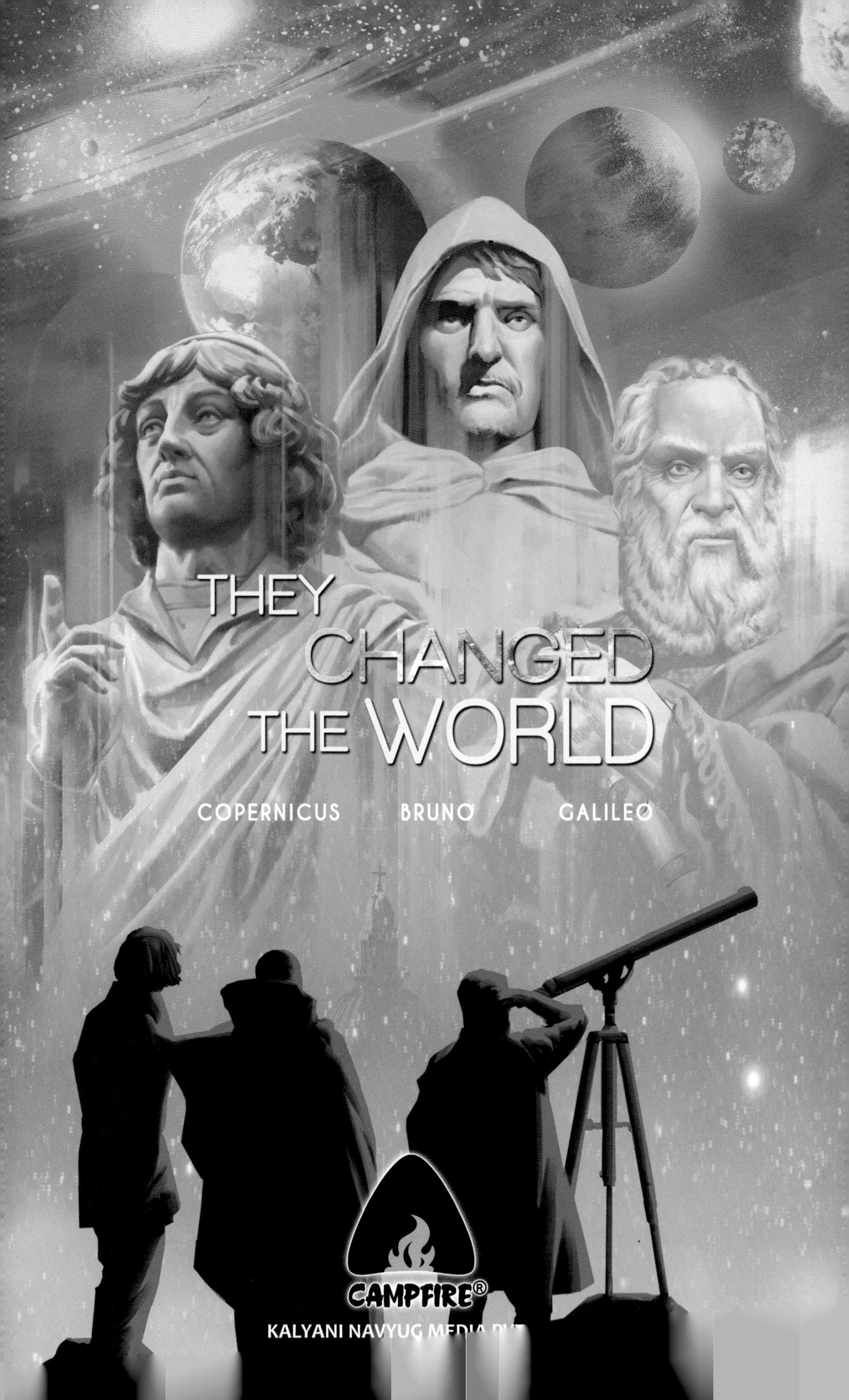
THEY CHANGED THE WORLD
COPERNICUS
BRUNO
GALILEO
CAMPFIRE®
KALYANI NAVYUG

CHAPTER 1

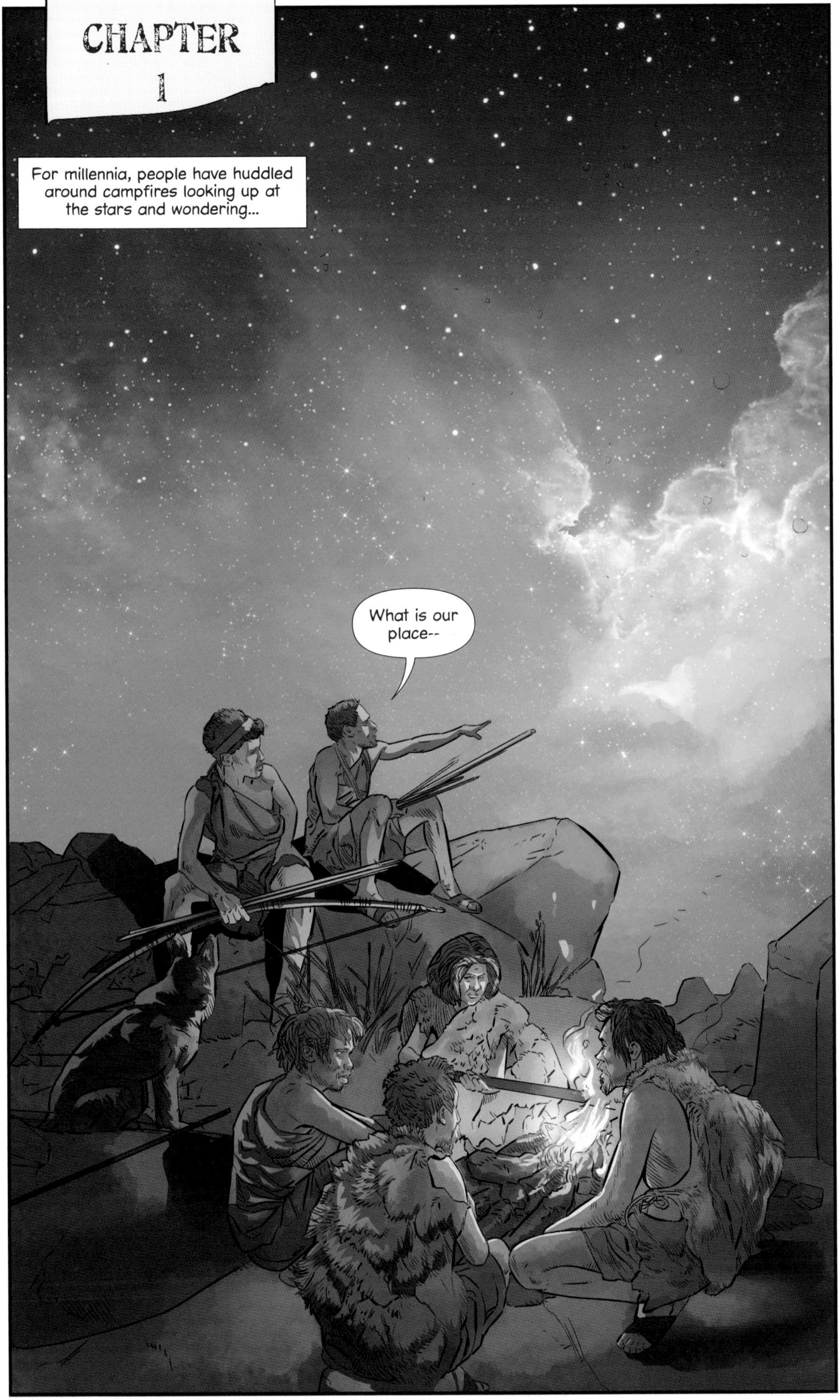
For millennia, people have huddled around campfires looking up at the stars and wondering...
What is our place--

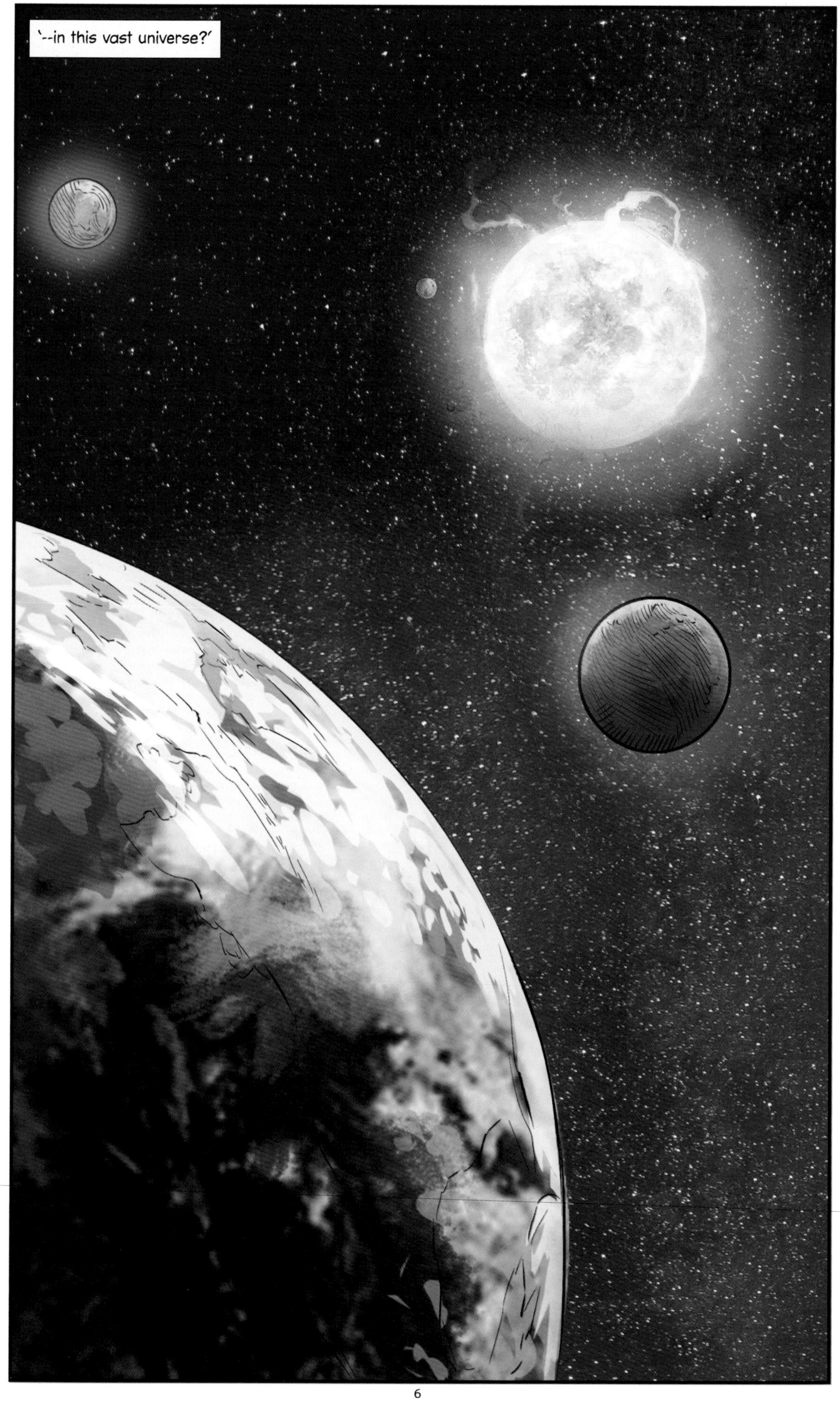
'--in this vast universe?'

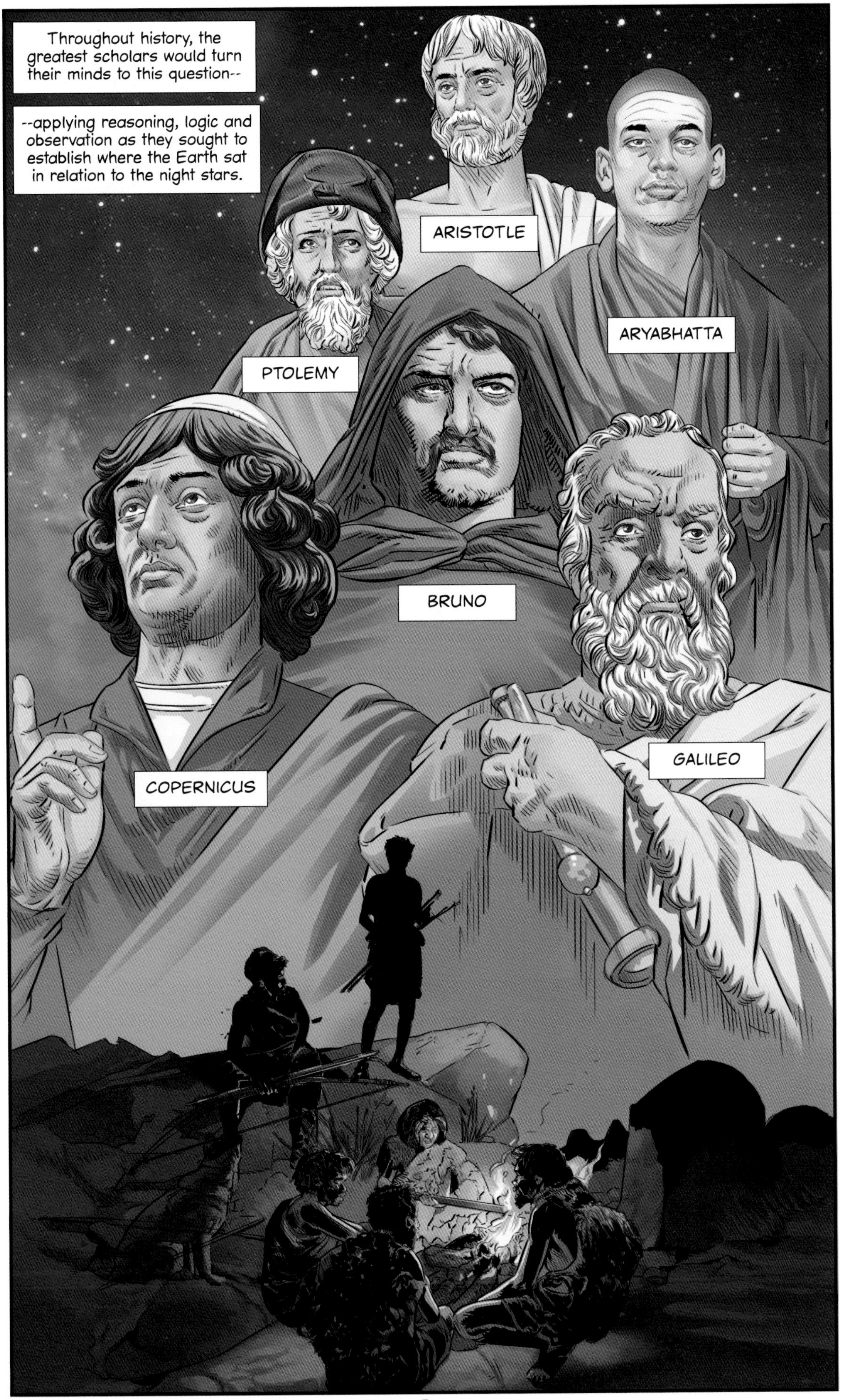
Throughout history, the greatest scholars would turn their minds to this question--
--applying reasoning, logic and observation as they sought to establish where the Earth sat in relation to the night stars.
ARISTOTLE
ARYABHATTA
PTOLEMY
BRUNO
COPERNICUS
GALILEO

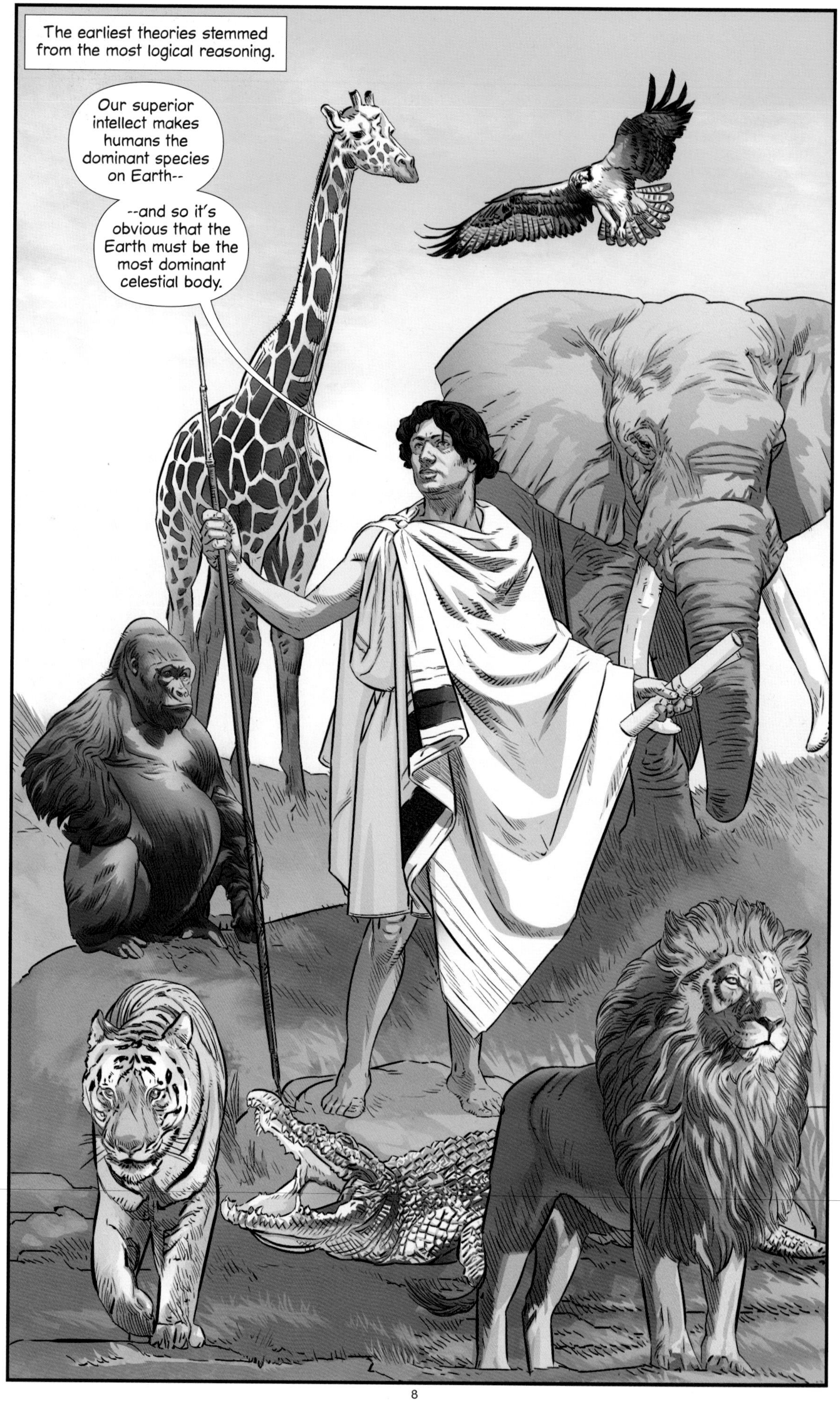
The earliest theories stemmed from the most logical reasoning.
Our superior intellect makes humans the dominant species on Earth--
--and so it's obvious that the Earth must be the most dominant celestial body.

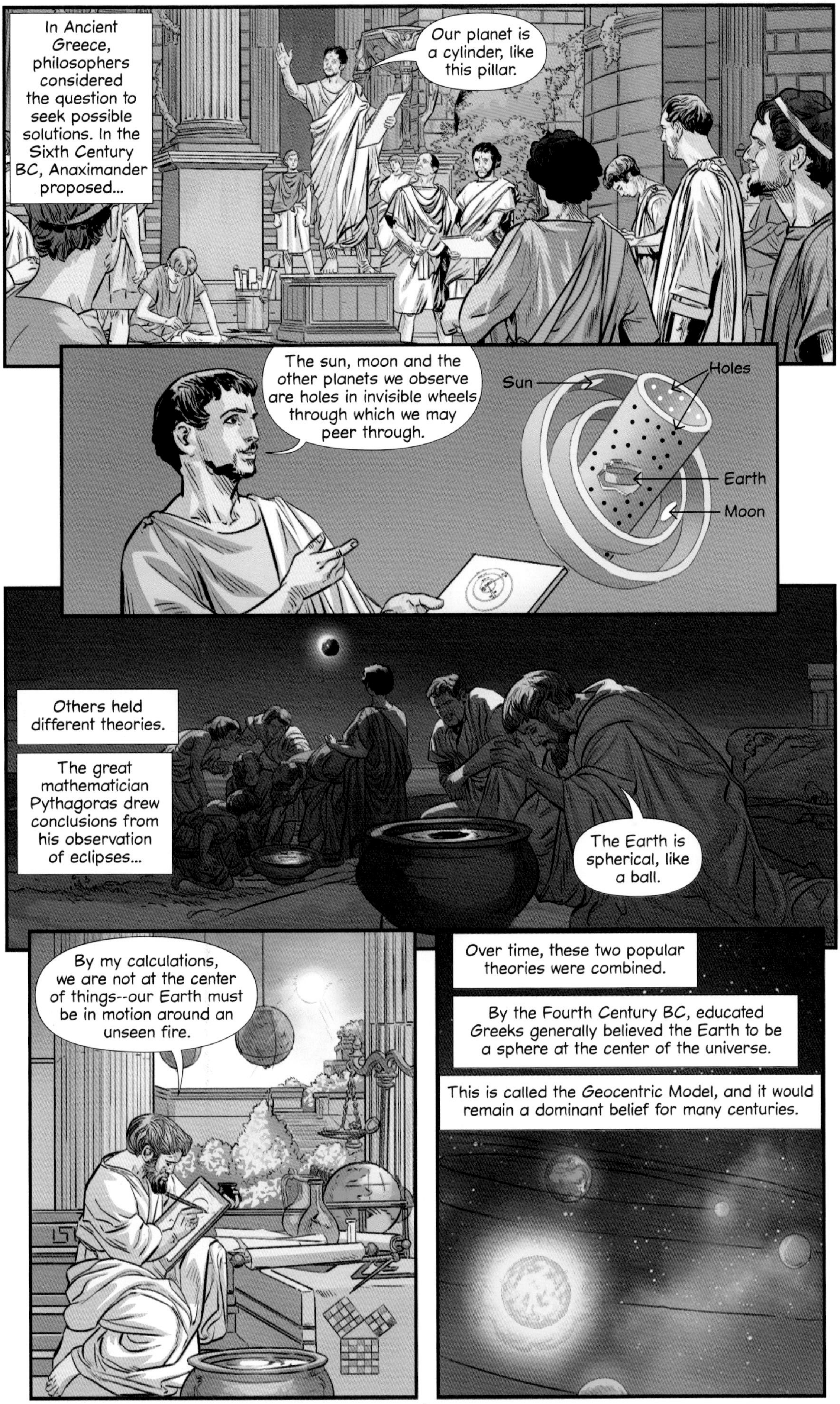
In Ancient Greece, philosophers considered the question to seek possible solutions. In the Sixth Century BC, Anaximander proposed...
Our planet is a cylinder, like this pillar.
The sun, moon and the other planets we observe are holes in invisible wheels through which we may peer through.
Sun
Holes
Earth
Moon
Others held different theories.
The great mathematician Pythagoras drew conclusions from his observation of eclipses...
The Earth is spherical, like a ball.
By my calculations, we are not at the center of things--our Earth must be in motion around an unseen fire.
Over time, these two popular theories were combined.
By the Fourth Century BC, educated Greeks generally believed the Earth to be a sphere at the center of the universe.
This is called the Geocentric Model, and it would remain a dominant belief for many centuries.

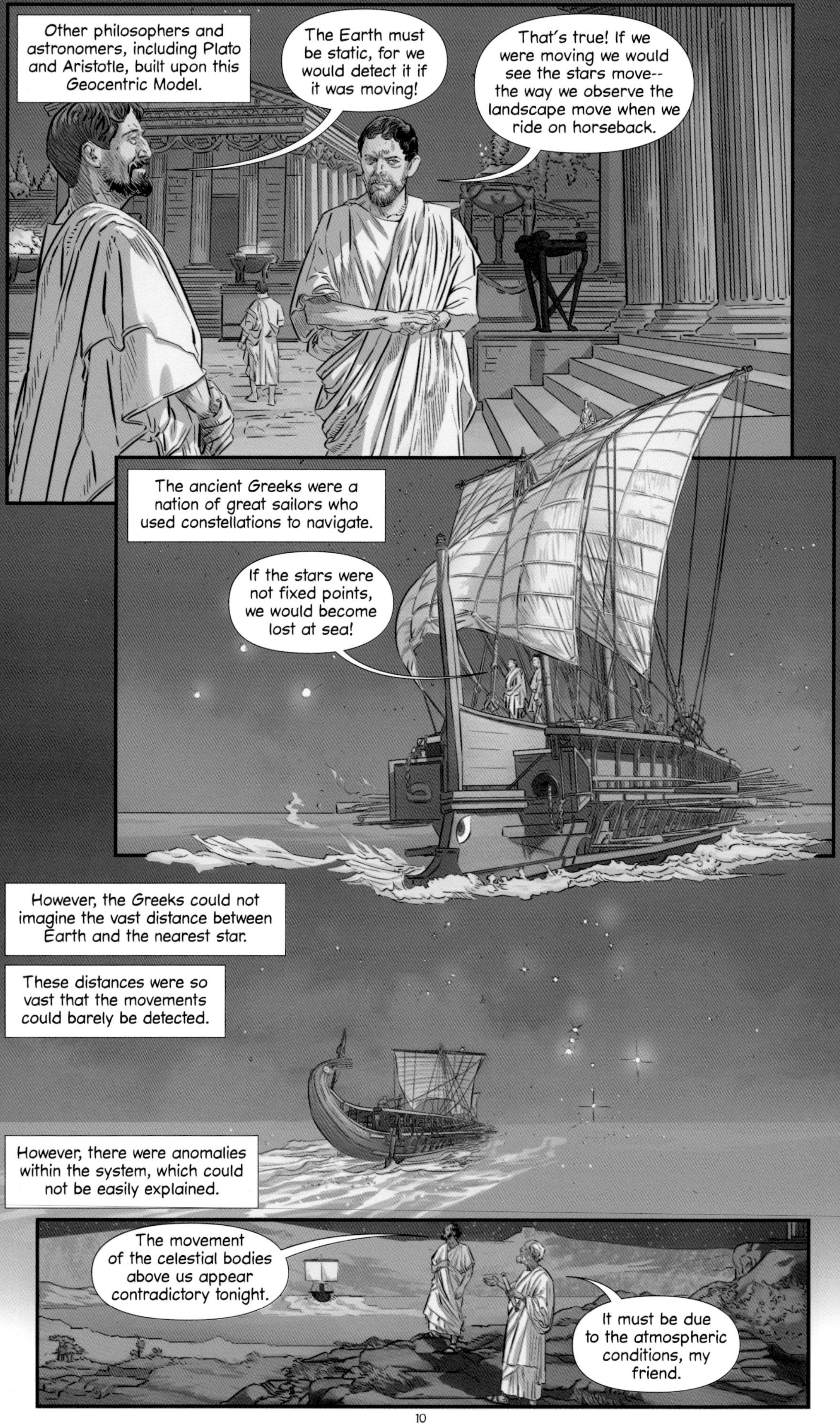
Other philosophers and astronomers, including Plato and Aristotle, built upon this Geocentric Model.
The Earth must be static, for we would detect it if it was moving!
That's true! If we were moving we would see the stars move-- the way we observe the landscape move when we ride on horseback.
The ancient Greeks were a nation of great sailors who used constellations to navigate.
If the stars were not fixed points, we would become lost at sea!
However, the Greeks could not imagine the vast distance between Earth and the nearest star.
These distances were so vast that the movements could barely be detected.
However, there were anomalies within the system, which could not be easily explained.
The movement of the celestial bodies above us appear contradictory tonight.
It must be due to the atmospheric conditions, my friend.

In the Second Century AD, Claudius Ptolemy of Alexandria - a part of the Roman Empire - set about refining the previous models.

The celestial movements we see can be explained by mathematics--

--but our mathematics must be employed in advanced ways.

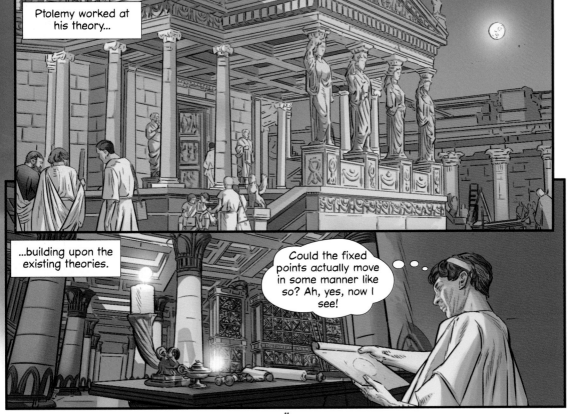

Ptolemy worked at his theory...

...building upon the existing theories.

Could the fixed points actually move in some manner like so? Ah, yes, now I see!

Ptolemy's elaborate model proposed that all celestial bodies were moving according to a system of two interlinked spheres, known as the deferent and the epicycle.

The deferent circle's central point was the eccentric, creating a kind of "wobble" whose varying distance from the Earth accounted for our different observations during the seasons.

The epicycle, meanwhile, provided the center around which the celestial body itself then moved, so that the planet moved within a circle and it was this circle which orbited the Earth.

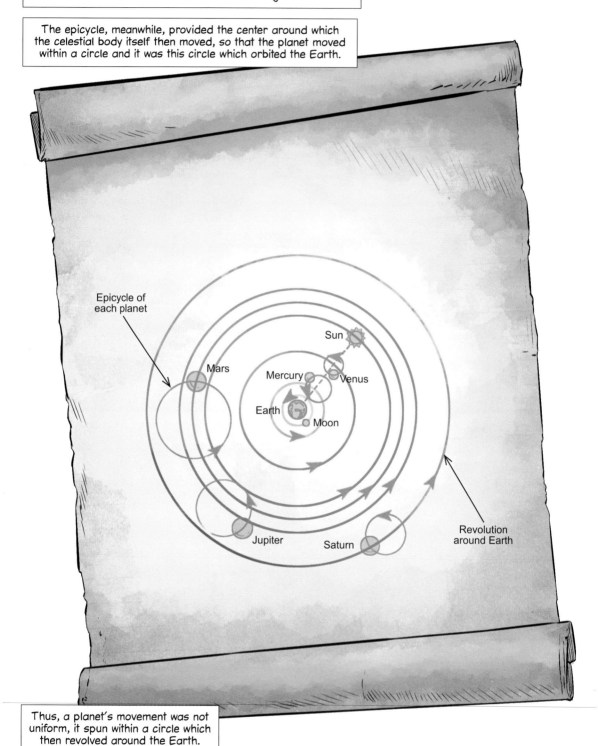

Epicycle of each planet

Sun

Mars

Mercury

Venus

Earth

Moon

Revolution around Earth

Jupiter

Saturn

Thus, a planet's movement was not uniform, it spun within a circle which then revolved around the Earth.

By this mechanism of "circles within circles", the slight variations of the planetary distances over time were accounted for.

Known as the Ptolemaic system, this model provided a satisfactory explanation for the elliptical orbits which the planets were observed to follow and was widely accepted.

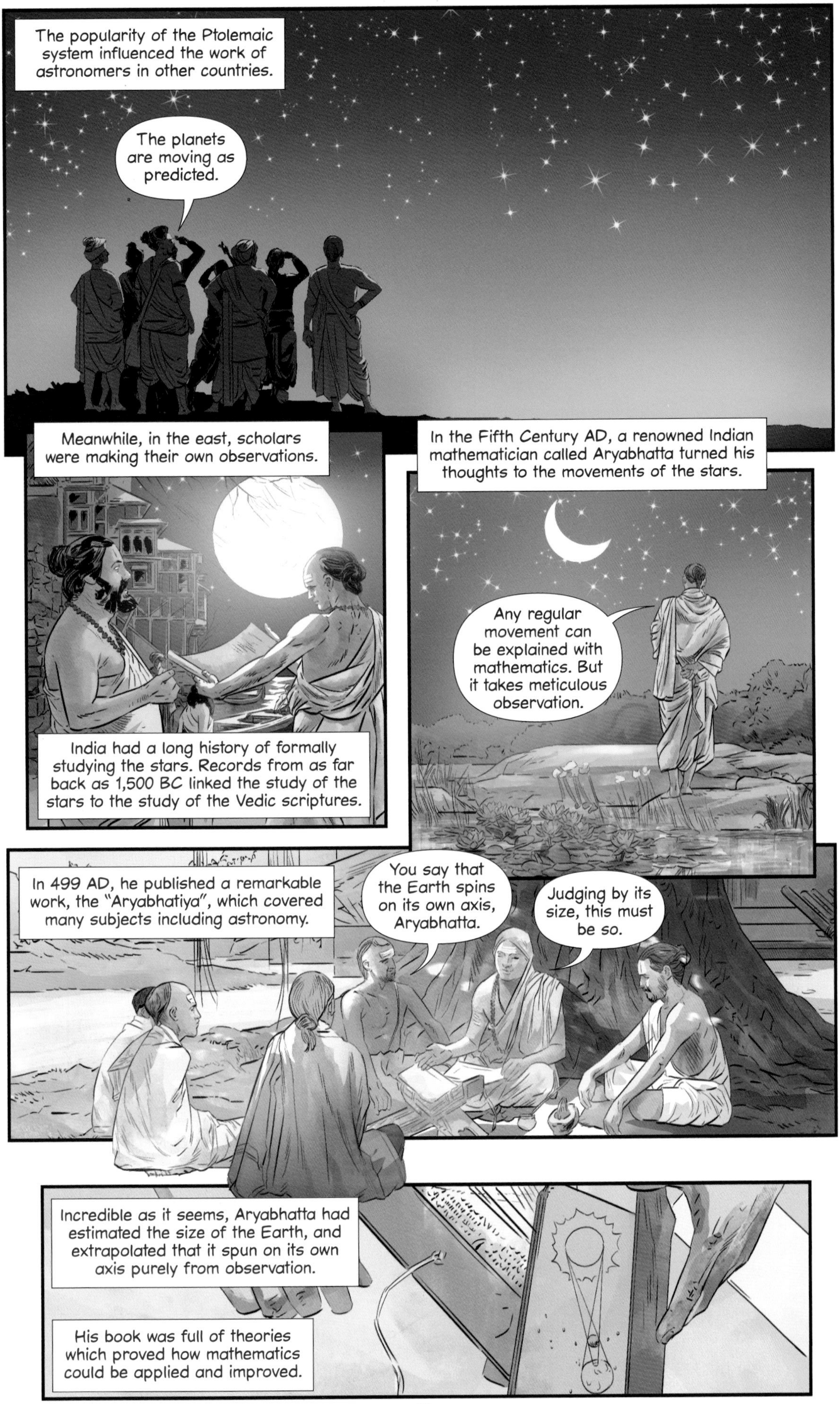
The popularity of the Ptolemaic system influenced the work of astronomers in other countries.
The planets are moving as predicted.
Meanwhile, in the east, scholars were making their own observations.
India had a long history of formally studying the stars. Records from as far back as 1,500 BC linked the study of the stars to the study of the Vedic scriptures.
In the Fifth Century AD, a renowned Indian mathematician called Aryabhatta turned his thoughts to the movements of the stars.
Any regular movement can be explained with mathematics. But it takes meticulous observation.
In 499 AD, he published a remarkable work, the "Aryabhatiya", which covered many subjects including astronomy.
You say that the Earth spins on its own axis, Aryabhatta.
Judging by its size, this must be so.
Incredible as it seems, Aryabhatta had estimated the size of the Earth, and extrapolated that it spun on its own axis purely from observation.
His book was full of theories which proved how mathematics could be applied and improved.

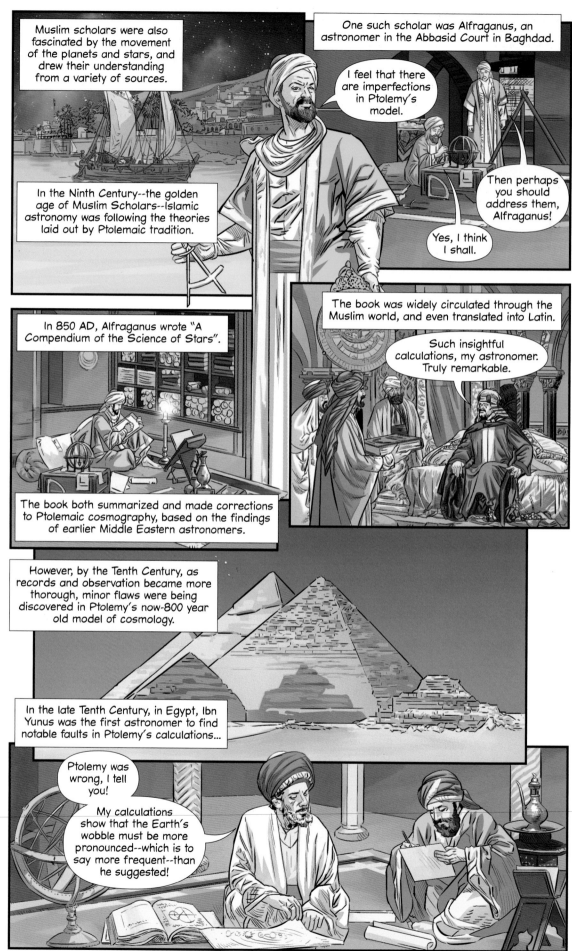

Muslim scholars were also fascinated by the movement of the planets and stars, and drew their understanding from a variety of sources.

In the Ninth Century--the golden age of Muslim Scholars--Islamic astronomy was following the theories laid out by Ptolemaic tradition.

One such scholar was Alfraganus, an astronomer in the Abbasid Court in Baghdad.

I feel that there are imperfections in Ptolemy's model.

Then perhaps you should address them, Alfraganus!

Yes, I think I shall.

In 850 AD, Alfraganus wrote "A Compendium of the Science of Stars".

The book both summarized and made corrections to Ptolemaic cosmography, based on the findings of earlier Middle Eastern astronomers.

The book was widely circulated through the Muslim world, and even translated into Latin.

Such insightful calculations, my astronomer. Truly remarkable.

However, by the Tenth Century, as records and observation became more thorough, minor flaws were being discovered in Ptolemy's now-800 year old model of cosmology.

In the late Tenth Century, in Egypt, Ibn Yunus was the first astronomer to find notable faults in Ptolemy's calculations...

Ptolemy was wrong, I tell you!

My calculations show that the Earth's wobble must be more pronounced--which is to say more frequent--than he suggested!

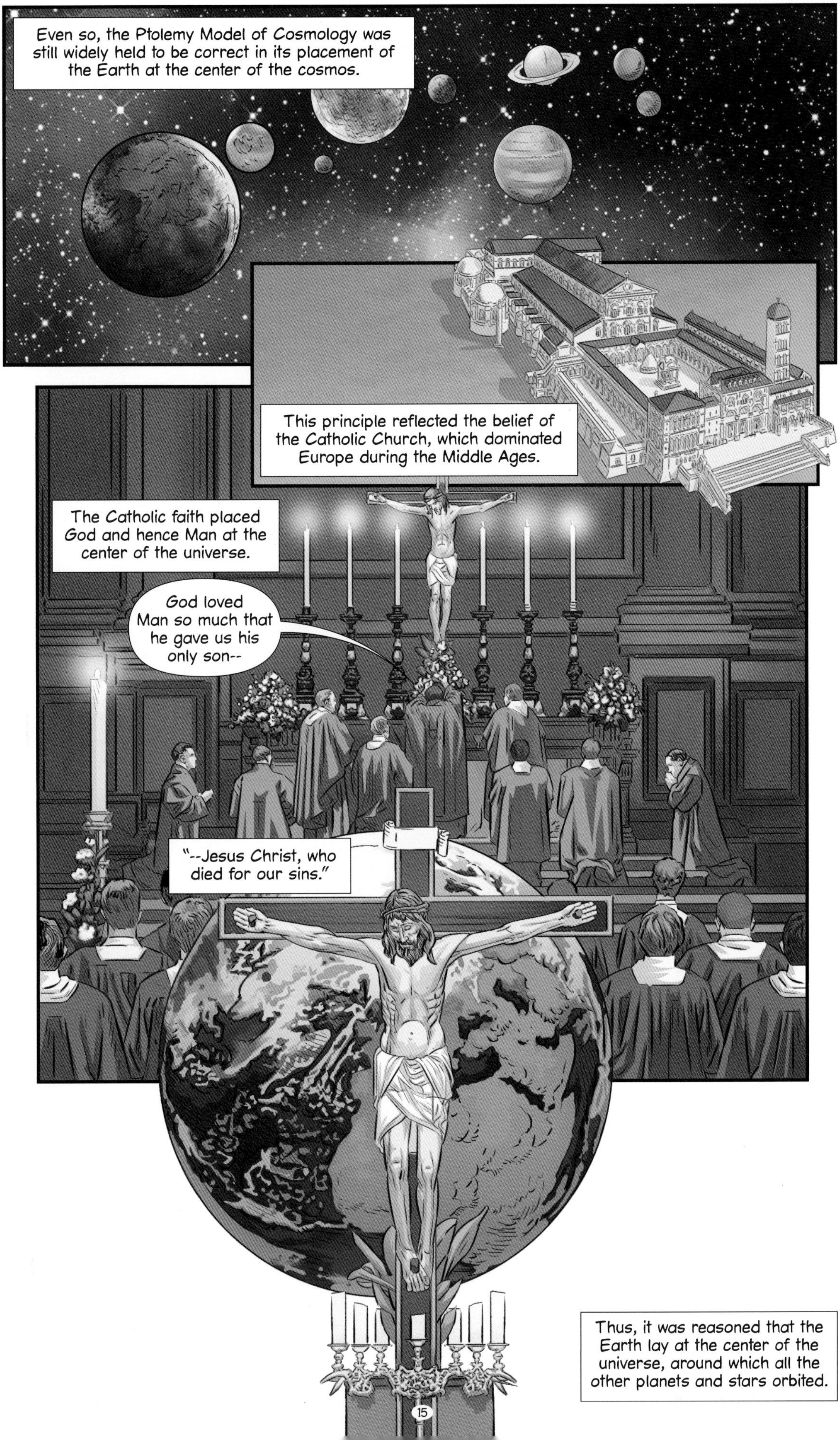
Even so, the Ptolemy Model of Cosmology was still widely held to be correct in its placement of the Earth at the center of the cosmos.
This principle reflected the belief of the Catholic Church, which dominated Europe during the Middle Ages.
The Catholic faith placed God and hence Man at the center of the universe.
God loved Man so much that he gave us his only son--
"--Jesus Christ, who died for our sins."
Thus, it was reasoned that the Earth lay at the center of the universe, around which all the other planets and stars orbited.

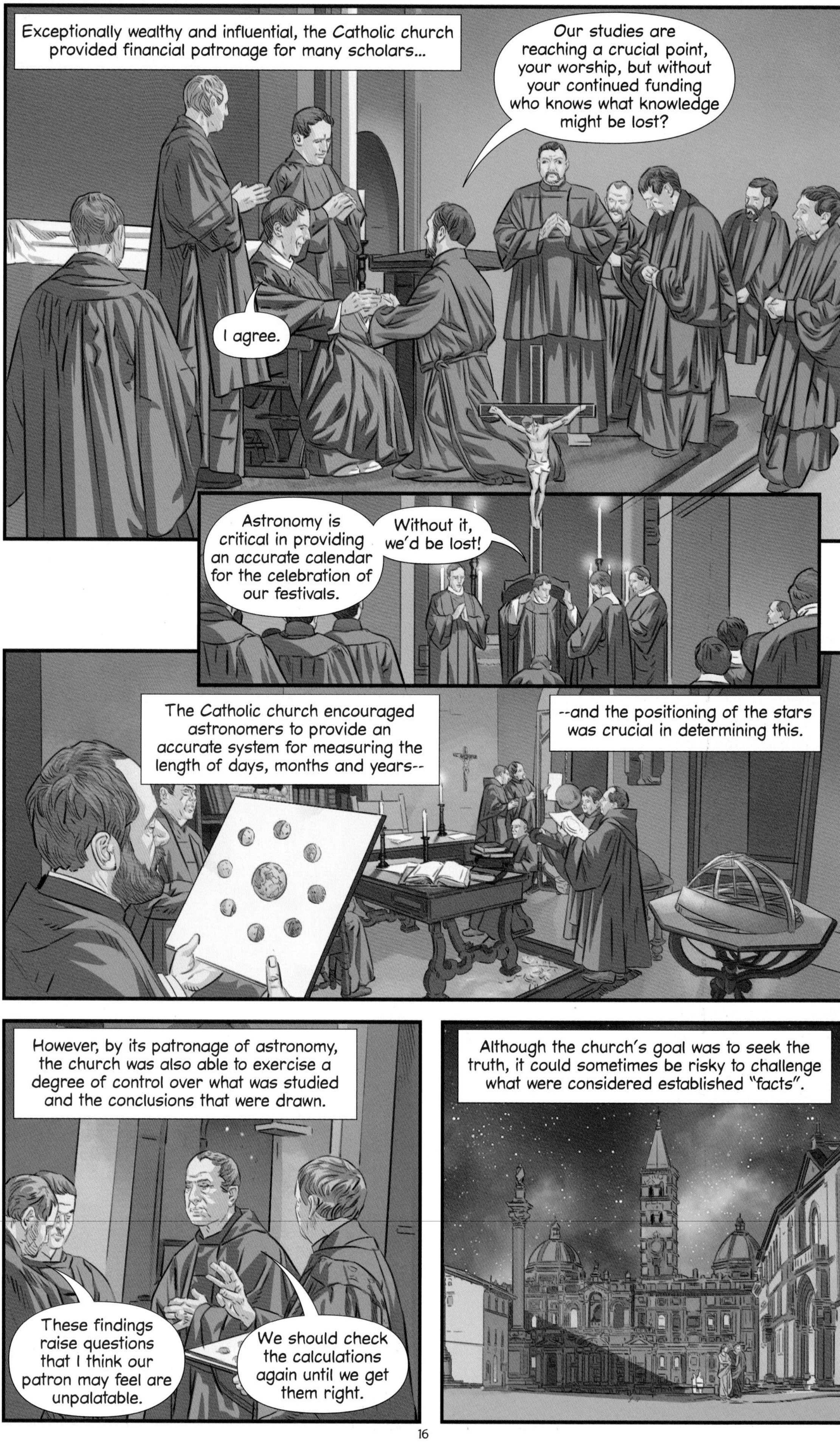
Exceptionally wealthy and influential, the Catholic church provided financial patronage for many scholars...
Our studies are reaching a crucial point, your worship, but without your continued funding who knows what knowledge might be lost?
I agree.
Astronomy is critical in providing an accurate calendar for the celebration of our festivals.
Without it, we'd be lost!
The Catholic church encouraged astronomers to provide an accurate system for measuring the length of days, months and years--
--and the positioning of the stars was crucial in determining this.
However, by its patronage of astronomy, the church was also able to exercise a degree of control over what was studied and the conclusions that were drawn.
These findings raise questions that I think our patron may feel are unpalatable.
We should check the calculations again until we get them right.
Although the church's goal was to seek the truth, it could sometimes be risky to challenge what were considered established "facts".

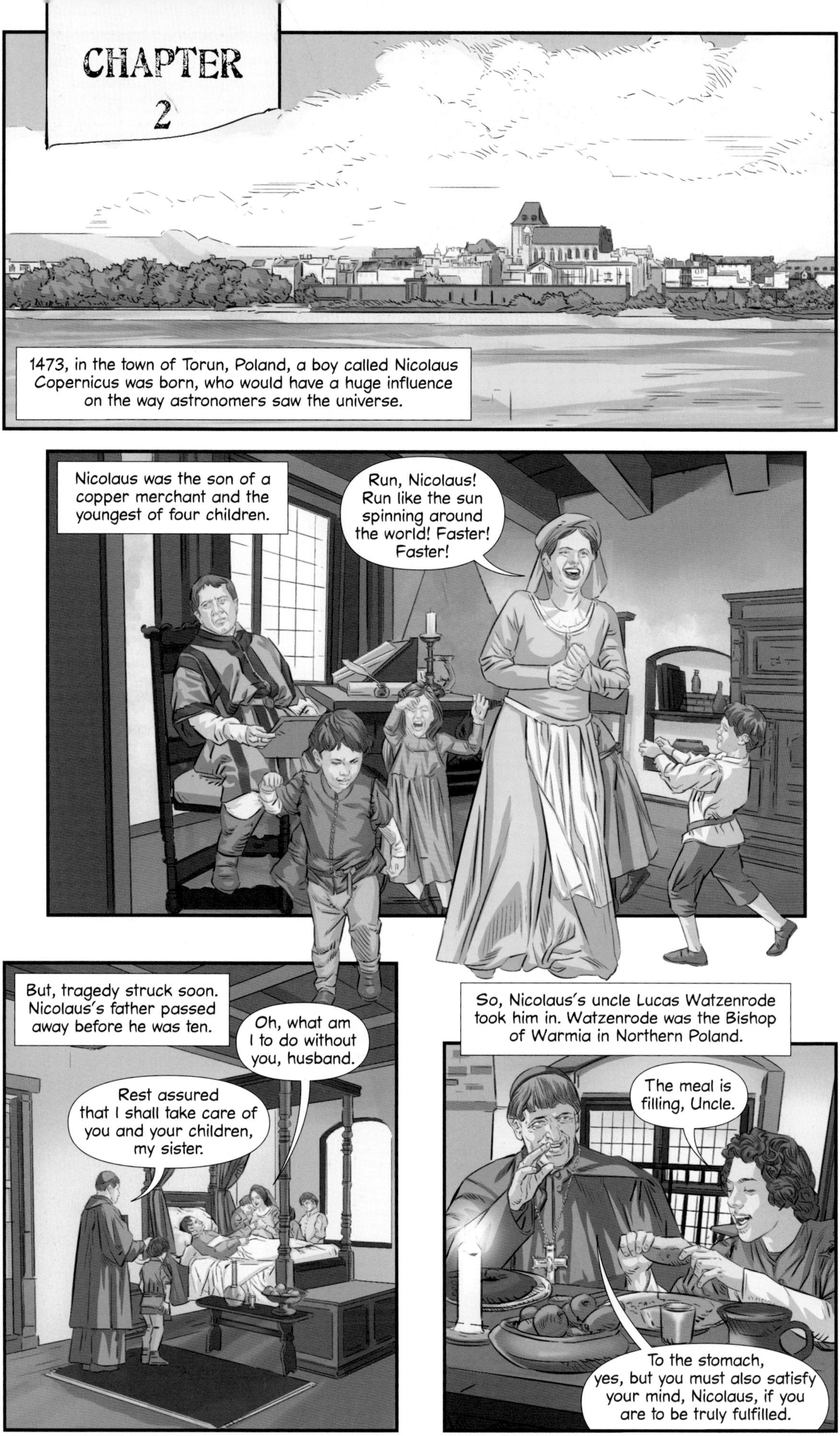
CHAPTER 2
1473, in the town of Torun, Poland, a boy called Nicolaus Copernicus was born, who would have a huge influence on the way astronomers saw the universe.
Nicolaus was the son of a copper merchant and the youngest of four children.
Run, Nicolaus! Run like the sun spinning around the world! Faster! Faster!
But, tragedy struck soon. Nicolaus's father passed away before he was ten.
Oh, what am I to do without you, husband.
Rest assured that I shall take care of you and your children, my sister.
So, Nicolaus's uncle Lucas Watzenrode took him in. Watzenrode was the Bishop of Warmia in Northern Poland.
The meal is filling, Uncle.
To the stomach, yes, but you must also satisfy your mind, Nicolaus, if you are to be truly fulfilled.

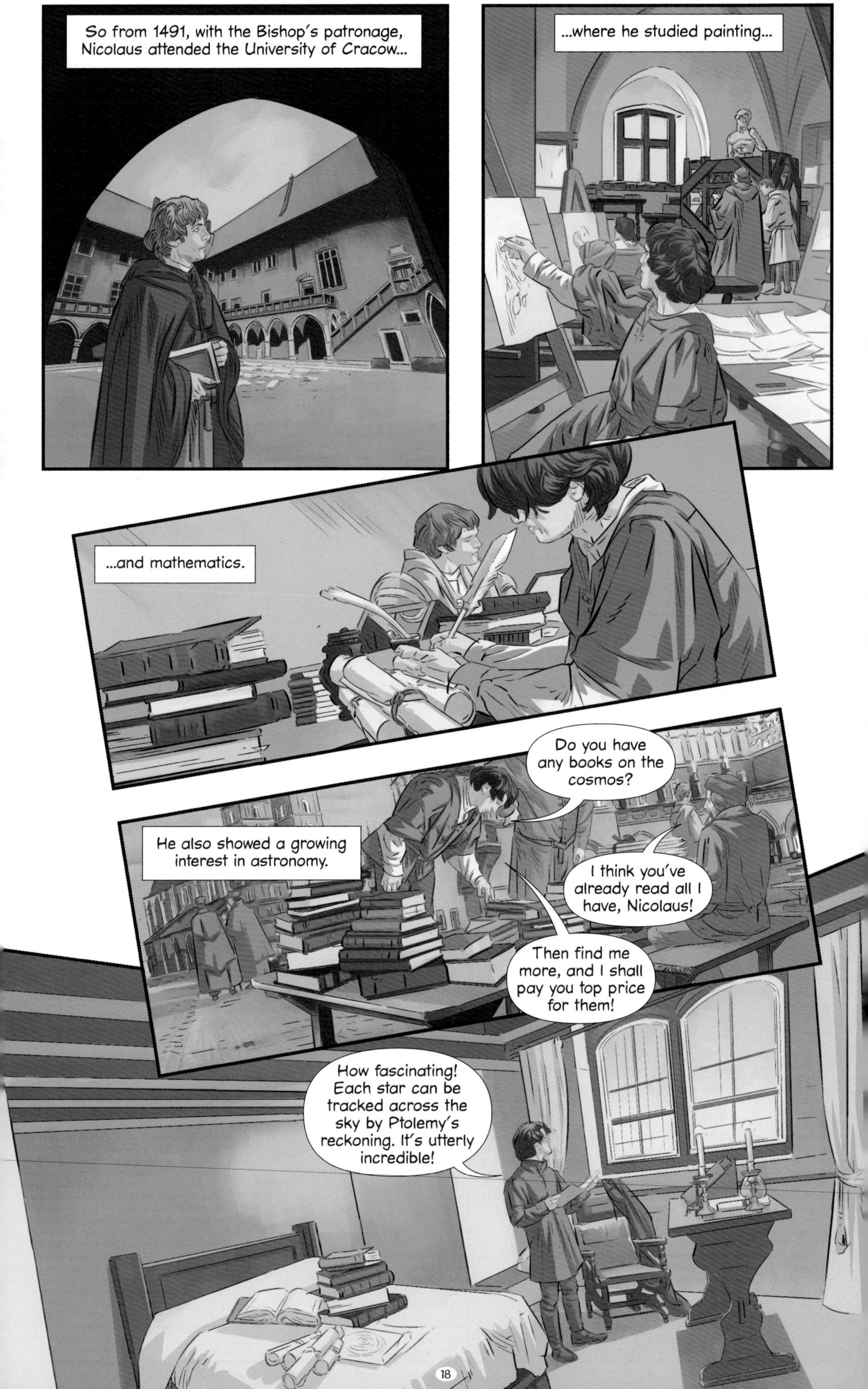
So from 1491, with the Bishop's patronage, Nicolaus attended the University of Cracow...
...where he studied painting...
...and mathematics.
He also showed a growing interest in astronomy.
Do you have any books on the cosmos?
I think you've already read all I have, Nicolaus!
Then find me more, and I shall pay you top price for them!
How fascinating! Each star can be tracked across the sky by Ptolemy's reckoning. It's utterly incredible!

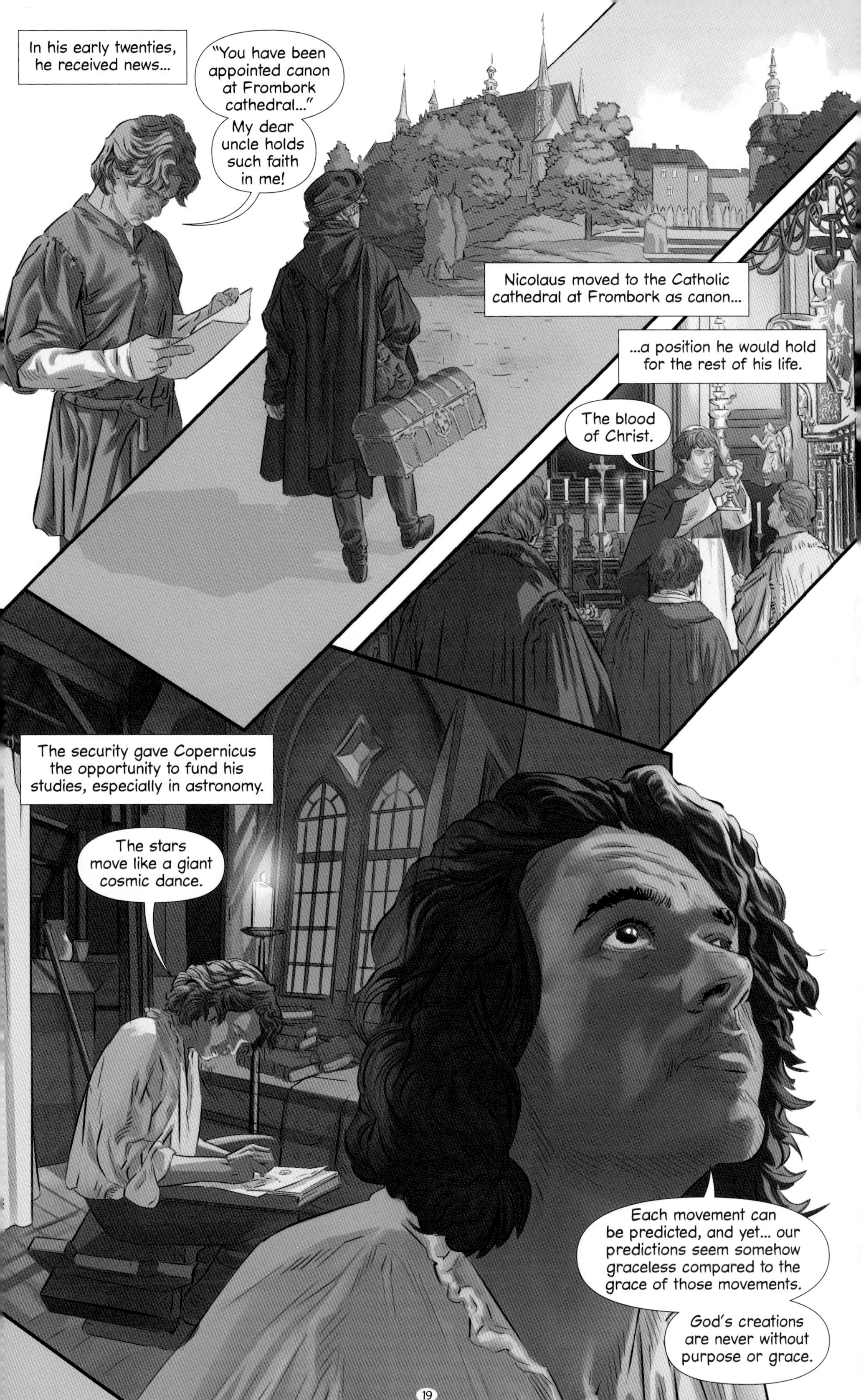
In his early twenties, he received news...
"You have been appointed canon at Frombork cathedral..."
My dear uncle holds such faith in me!
Nicolaus moved to the Catholic cathedral at Frombork as canon...
...a position he would hold for the rest of his life.
The blood of Christ.
The security gave Copernicus the opportunity to fund his studies, especially in astronomy.
The stars move like a giant cosmic dance.
Each movement can be predicted, and yet... our predictions seem somehow graceless compared to the grace of those movements.
God's creations are never without purpose or grace.

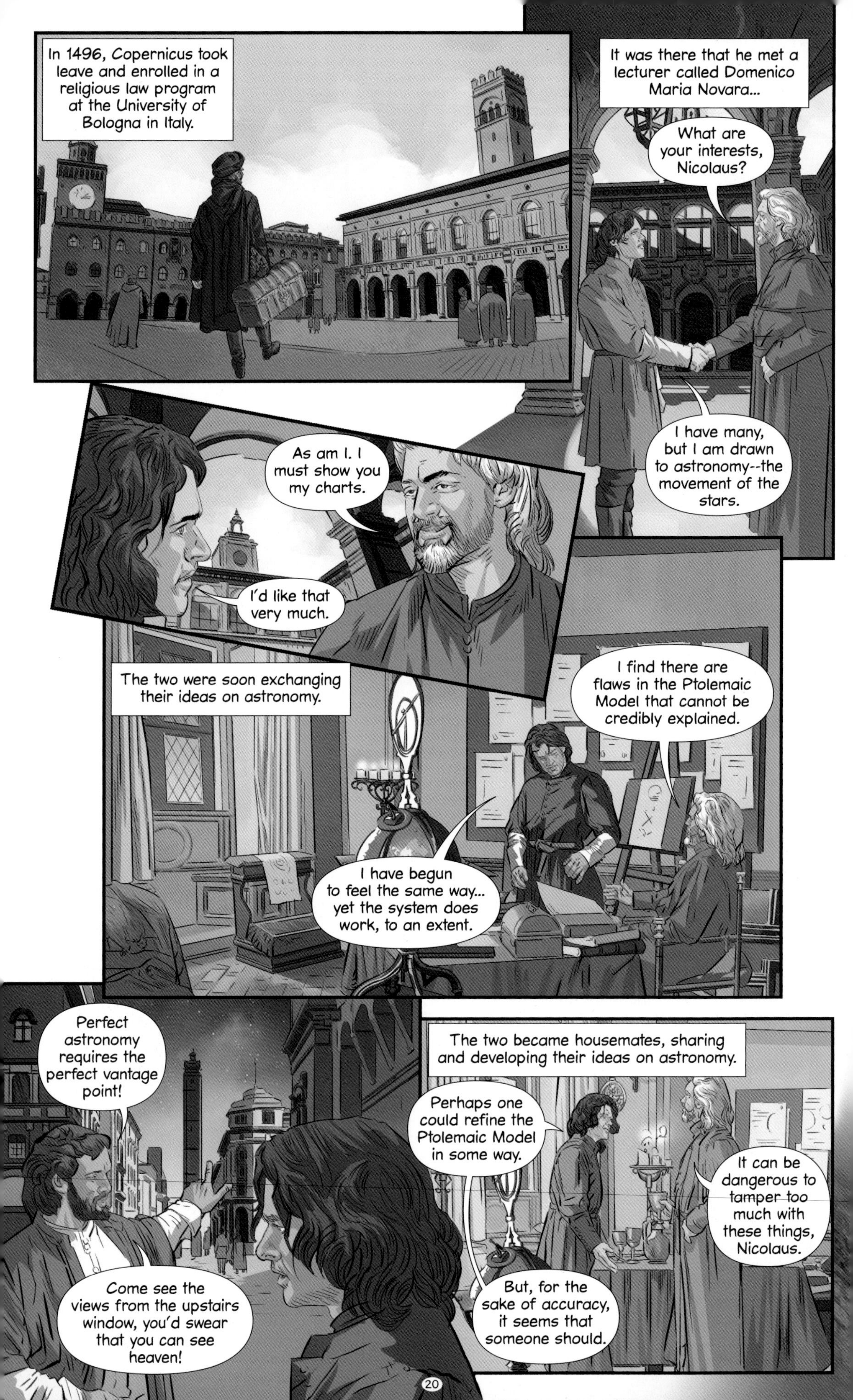
In 1496, Copernicus took leave and enrolled in a religious law program at the University of Bologna in Italy.
It was there that he met a lecturer called Domenico Maria Novara...
What are your interests, Nicolaus?
I have many, but I am drawn to astronomy--the movement of the stars.
As am I. I must show you my charts.
I'd like that very much.
The two were soon exchanging their ideas on astronomy.
I find there are flaws in the Ptolemaic Model that cannot be credibly explained.
I have begun to feel the same way... yet the system does work, to an extent.
Perfect astronomy requires the perfect vantage point!
Come see the views from the upstairs window, you'd swear that you can see heaven!
The two became housemates, sharing and developing their ideas on astronomy.
Perhaps one could refine the Ptolemaic Model in some way.
It can be dangerous to tamper too much with these things, Nicolaus.
But, for the sake of accuracy, it seems that someone should.

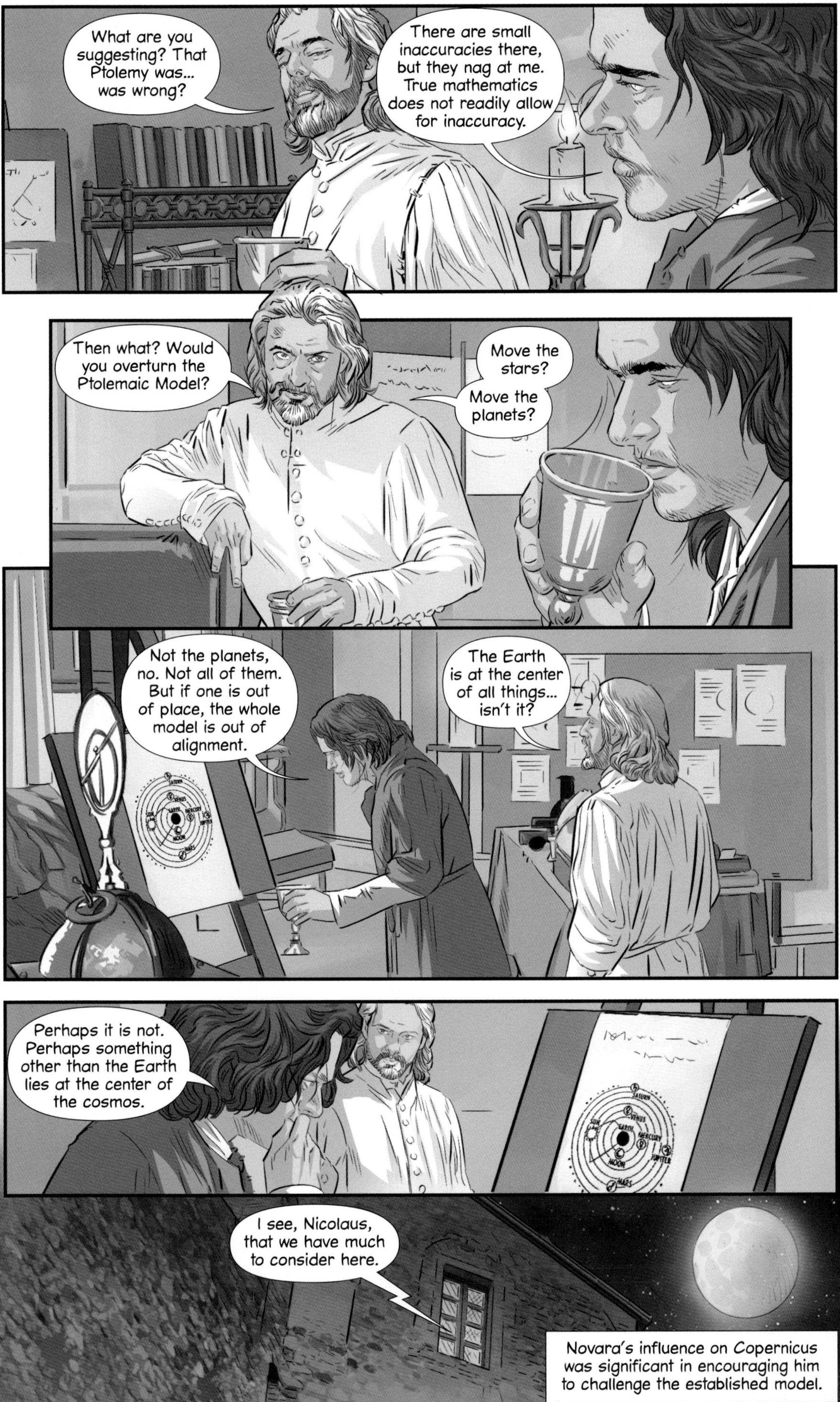
What are you suggesting? That Ptolemy was... was wrong?
There are small inaccuracies there, but they nag at me. True mathematics does not readily allow for inaccuracy.
Then what? Would you overturn the Ptolemaic Model?
Move the stars?
Move the planets?
Not the planets, no. Not all of them. But if one is out of place, the whole model is out of alignment.
The Earth is at the center of all things... isn't it?
Perhaps it is not. Perhaps something other than the Earth lies at the center of the cosmos.
SATURN
SUN
VENUS
EARTH
MERCURY
MOON
JUPITER
MARS
I see, Nicolaus, that we have much to consider here.
Novara's influence on Copernicus was significant in encouraging him to challenge the established model.

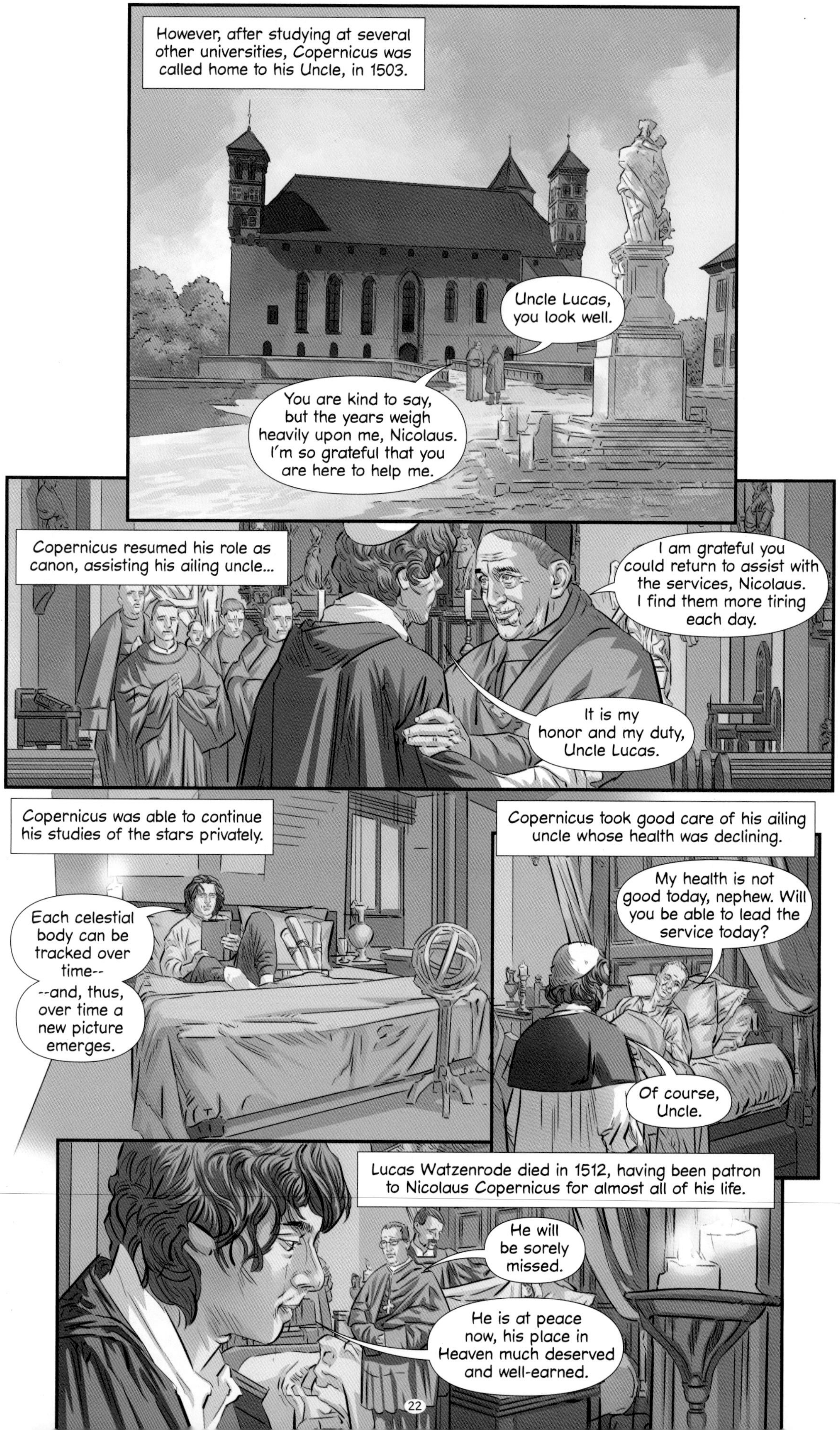

However, after studying at several other universities, Copernicus was called home to his Uncle, in 1503.
Uncle Lucas, you look well.
You are kind to say, but the years weigh heavily upon me, Nicolaus. I'm so grateful that you are here to help me.
Copernicus resumed his role as canon, assisting his ailing uncle...
I am grateful you could return to assist with the services, Nicolaus. I find them more tiring each day.
It is my honor and my duty, Uncle Lucas.
Copernicus was able to continue his studies of the stars privately.
Each celestial body can be tracked over time--
--and, thus, over time a new picture emerges.
Copernicus took good care of his ailing uncle whose health was declining.
My health is not good today, nephew. Will you be able to lead the service today?
Of course, Uncle.
Lucas Watzenrode died in 1512, having been patron to Nicolaus Copernicus for almost all of his life.
He will be sorely missed.
He is at peace now, his place in Heaven much deserved and well-earned.

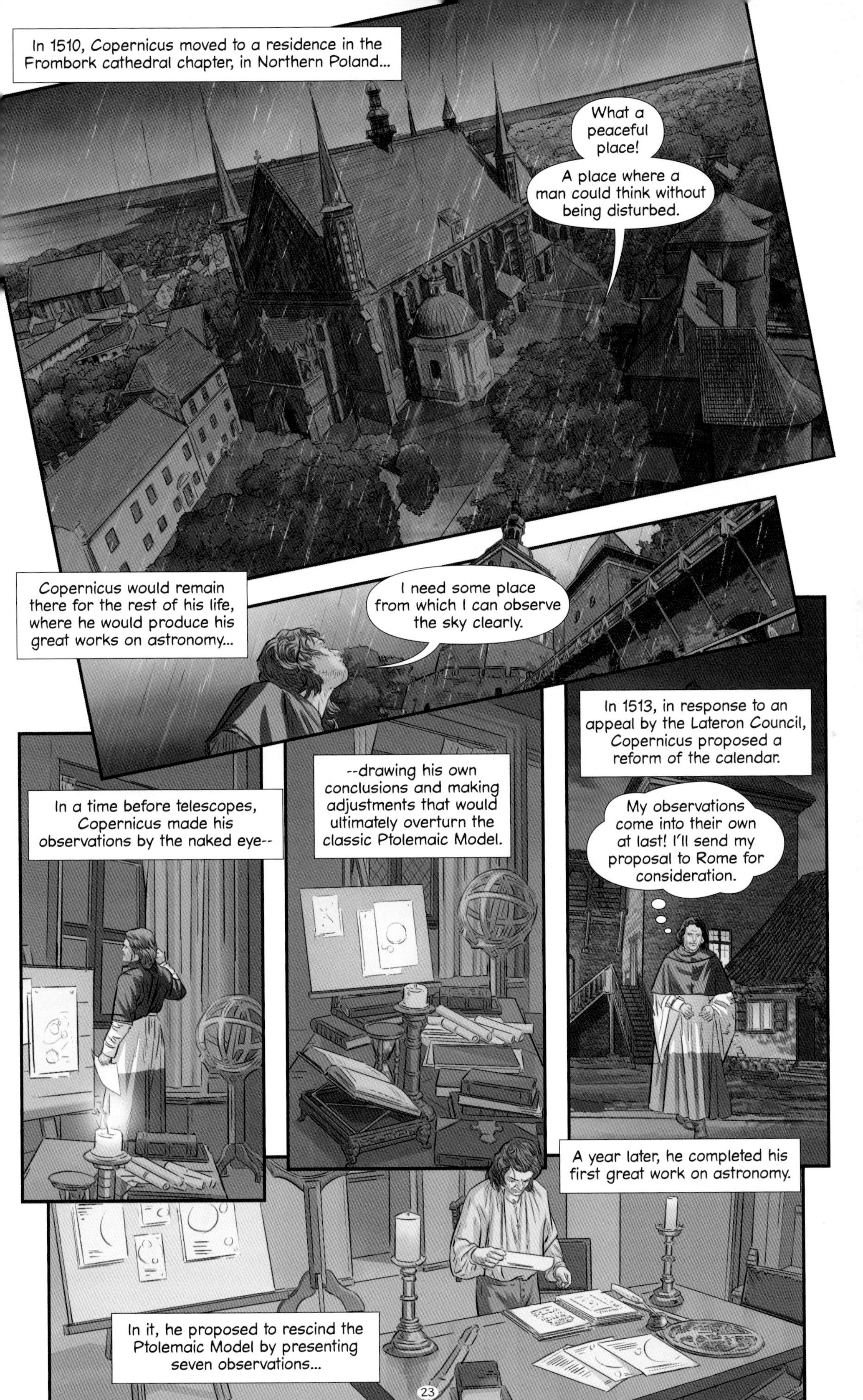
In 1510, Copernicus moved to a residence in the Frombork cathedral chapter, in Northern Poland...
What a peaceful place!
A place where a man could think without being disturbed.
Copernicus would remain there for the rest of his life, where he would produce his great works on astronomy...
I need some place from which I can observe the sky clearly.
In a time before telescopes, Copernicus made his observations by the naked eye--
--drawing his own conclusions and making adjustments that would ultimately overturn the classic Ptolemaic Model.
In 1513, in response to an appeal by the Lateron Council, Copernicus proposed a reform of the calendar.
My observations come into their own at last! I'll send my proposal to Rome for consideration.
A year later, he completed his first great work on astronomy.
In it, he proposed to rescind the Ptolemaic Model by presenting seven observations...

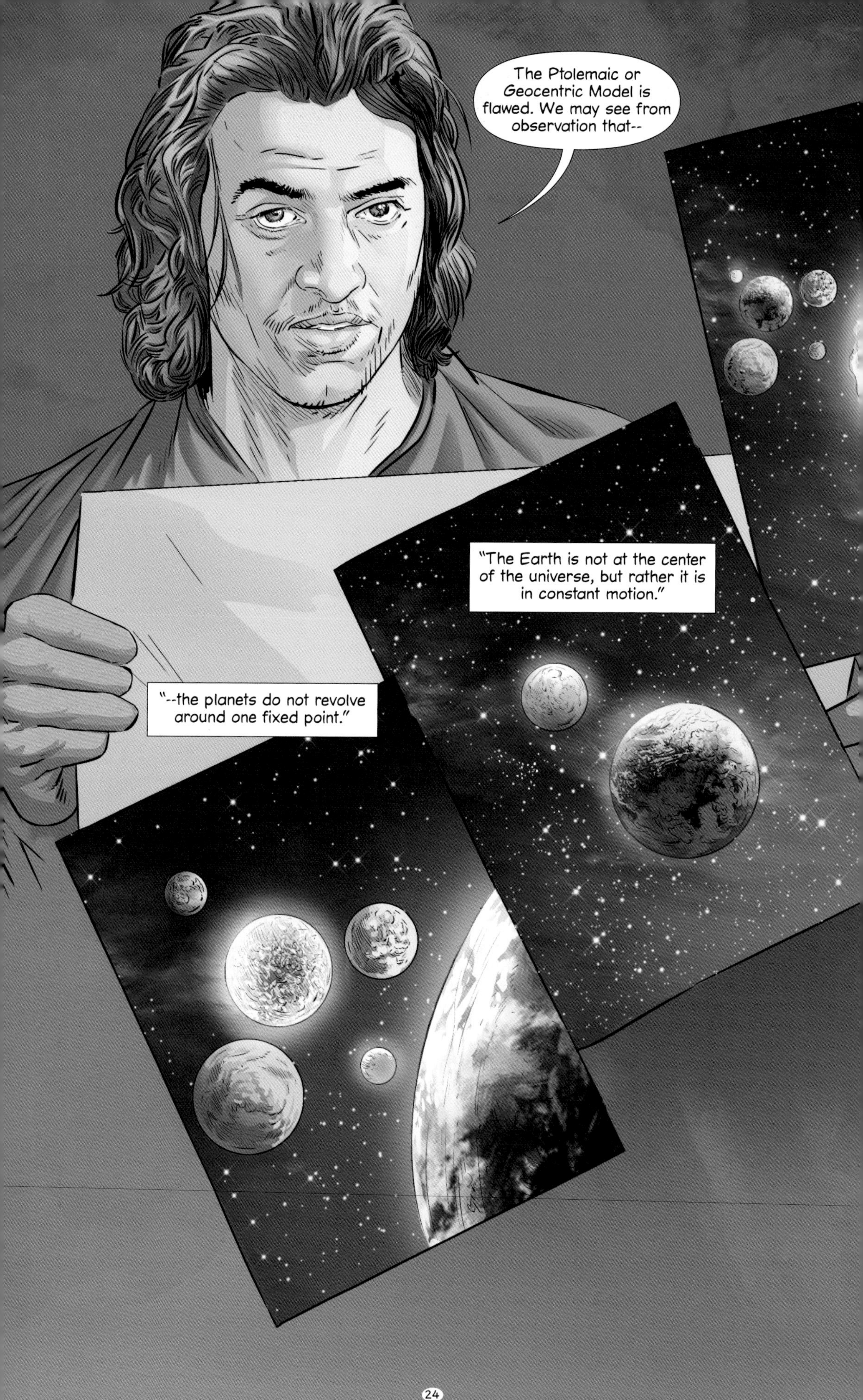
The Ptolemaic or Geocentric Model is flawed. We may see from observation that--
"The Earth is not at the center of the universe, but rather it is in constant motion."
"--the planets do not revolve around one fixed point."

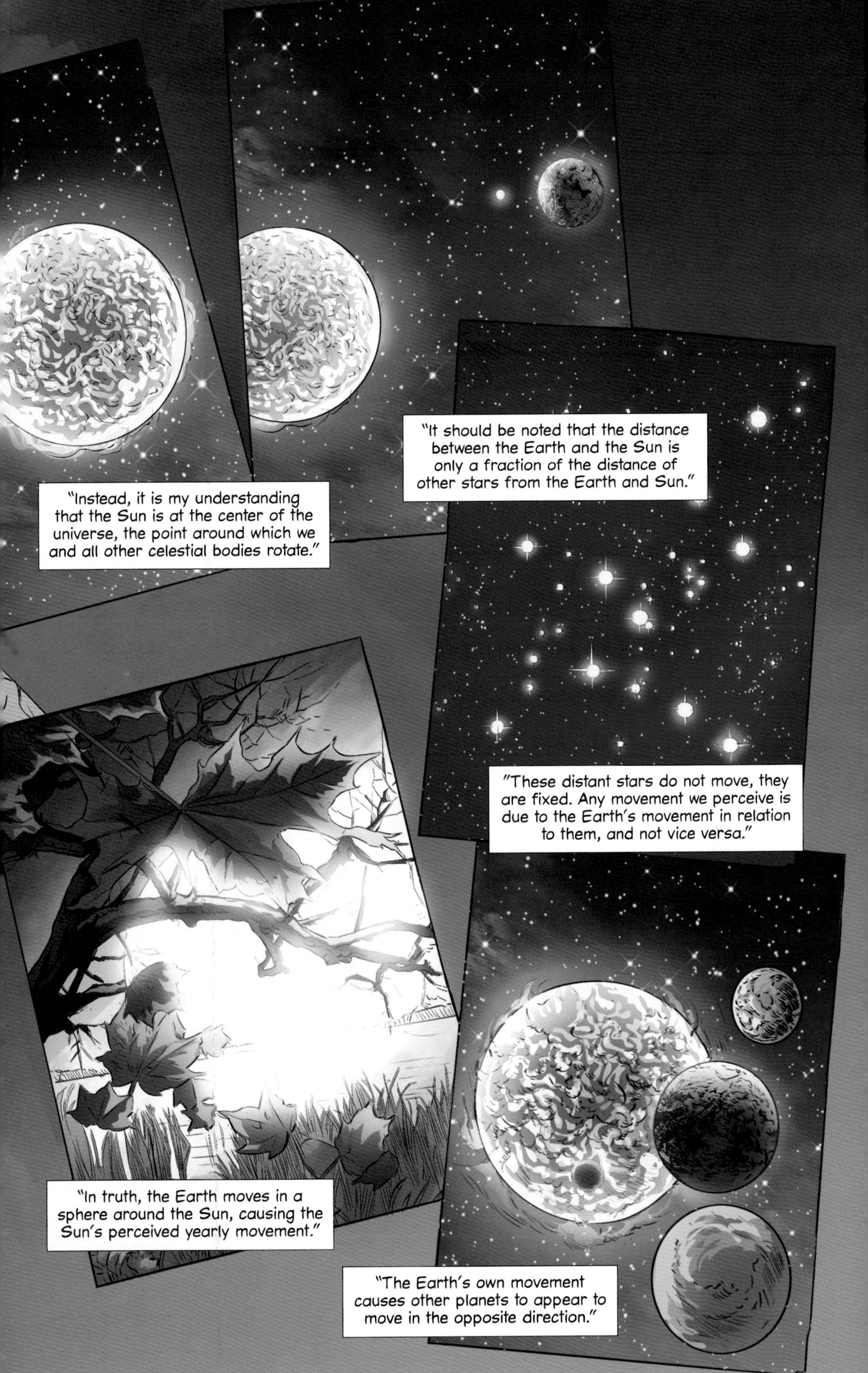
"Instead, it is my understanding that the Sun is at the center of the universe, the point around which we and all other celestial bodies rotate."
"It should be noted that the distance between the Earth and the Sun is only a fraction of the distance of other stars from the Earth and Sun."
"These distant stars do not move, they are fixed. Any movement we perceive is due to the Earth's movement in relation to them, and not vice versa."
"In truth, the Earth moves in a sphere around the Sun, causing the Sun's perceived yearly movement."
"The Earth's own movement causes other planets to appear to move in the opposite direction."

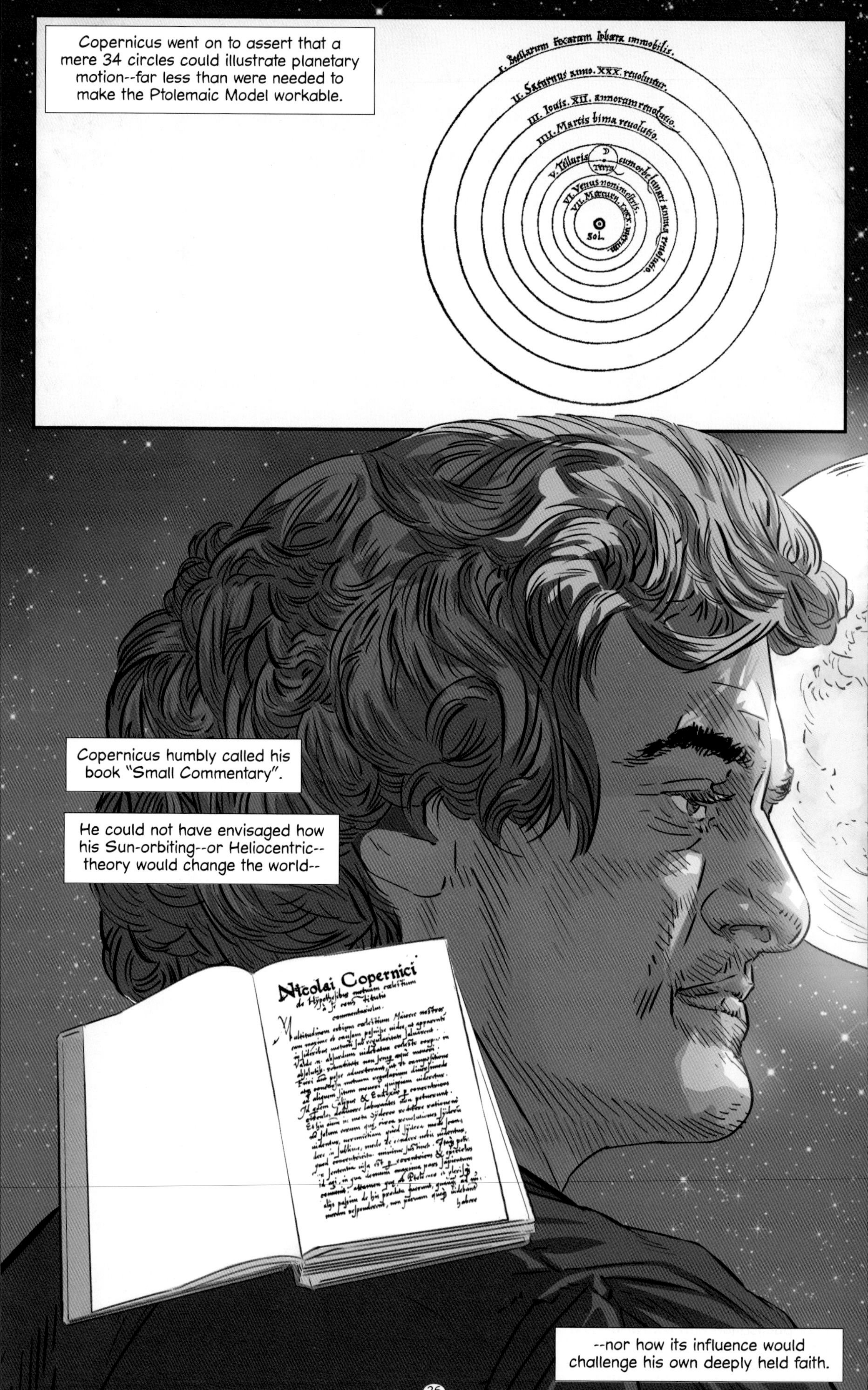

Copernicus went on to assert that a mere 34 circles could illustrate planetary motion--far less than were needed to make the Ptolemaic Model workable.
I. Stellarum fixarum sphaera immobilis.
II. Saturnus anno. XXX. revolvitur.
III. Iovis. XII. annorum revolutio.
IIII. Martis bima revolutio.
V. Telluris cum orbe lunari annua revolutio.
Terra
VI. Venus nono mense reducitur.
VII. Mercurius. LXXX. dierum.
Sol.
Copernicus humbly called his book "Small Commentary".
He could not have envisaged how his Sun-orbiting--or Heliocentric--theory would change the world--
Nicolai Copernici
--nor how its influence would challenge his own deeply held faith.

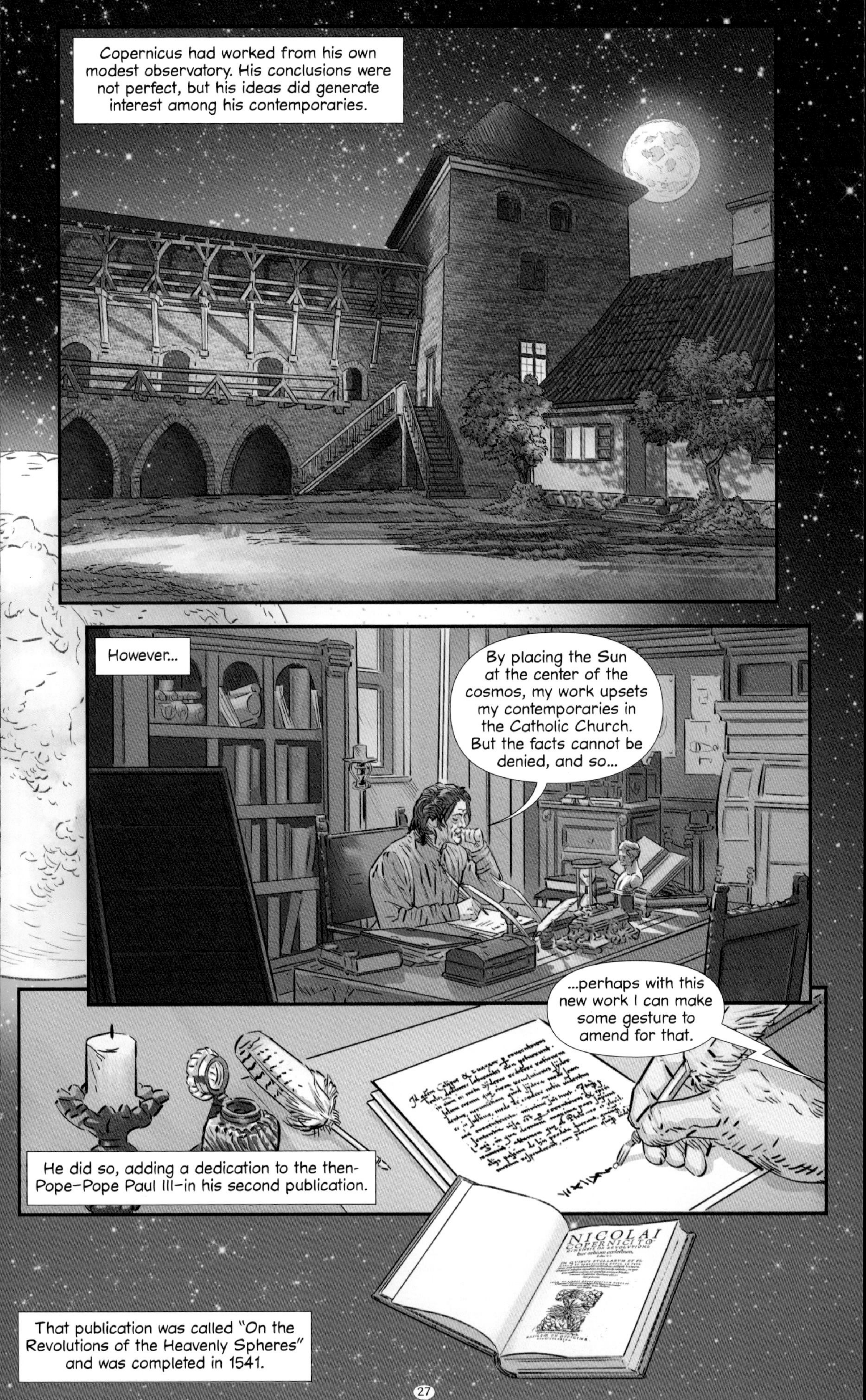
Copernicus had worked from his own modest observatory. His conclusions were not perfect, but his ideas did generate interest among his contemporaries.
However...
By placing the Sun at the center of the cosmos, my work upsets my contemporaries in the Catholic Church. But the facts cannot be denied, and so...
...perhaps with this new work I can make some gesture to amend for that.
He did so, adding a dedication to the then-Pope–Pope Paul III–in his second publication.
NICOLAI
That publication was called "On the Revolutions of the Heavenly Spheres" and was completed in 1541.

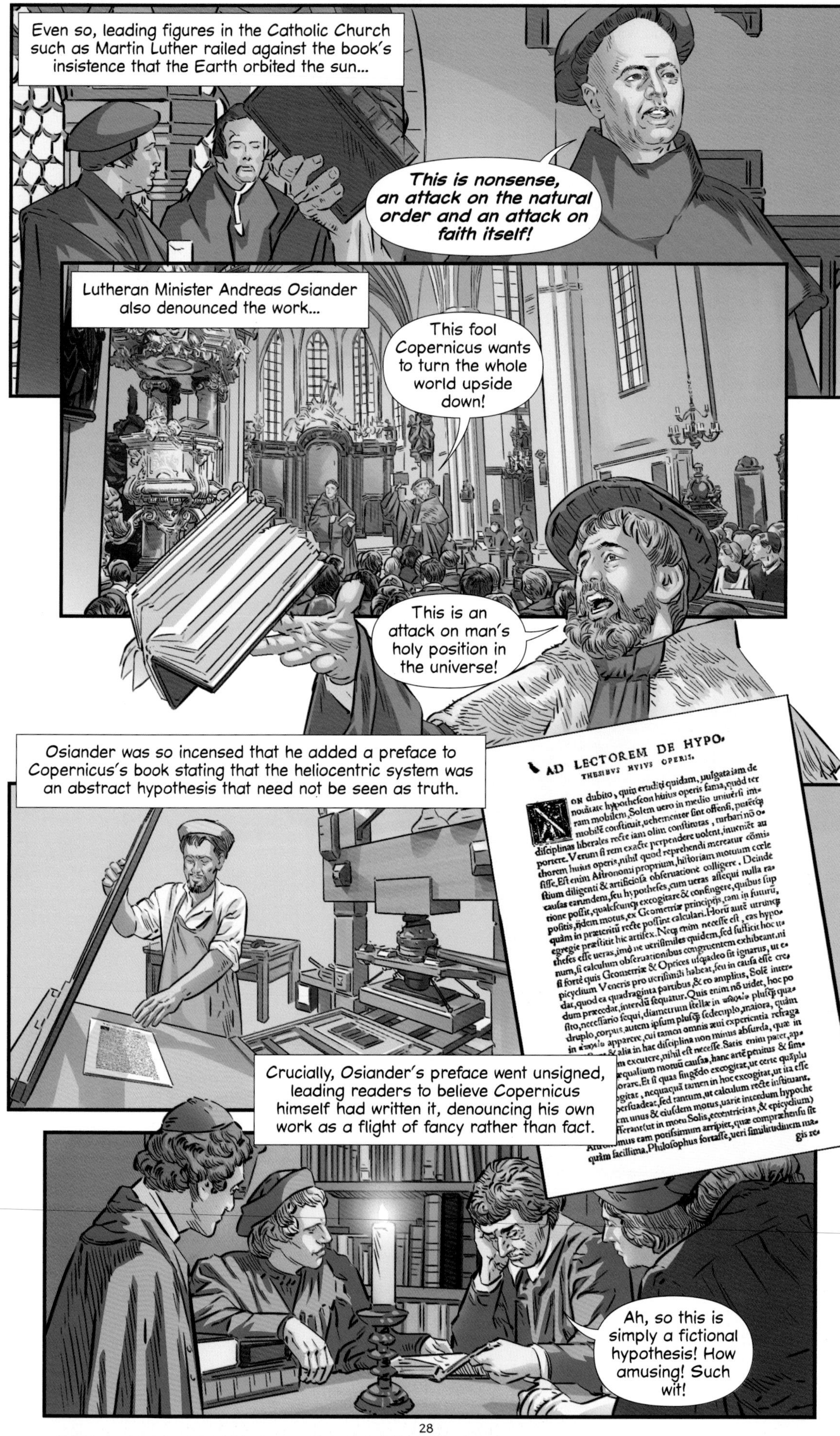
Even so, leading figures in the Catholic Church such as Martin Luther railed against the book's insistence that the Earth orbited the sun...
This is nonsense, an attack on the natural order and an attack on faith itself!
Lutheran Minister Andreas Osiander also denounced the work...
This fool Copernicus wants to turn the whole world upside down!
This is an attack on man's holy position in the universe!
Osiander was so incensed that he added a preface to Copernicus's book stating that the heliocentric system was an abstract hypothesis that need not be seen as truth.
AD LECTOREM DE HYPO-
THESIBVS HVIVS OPERIS.
Crucially, Osiander's preface went unsigned, leading readers to believe Copernicus himself had written it, denouncing his own work as a flight of fancy rather than fact.
Ah, so this is simply a fictional hypothesis! How amusing! Such wit!

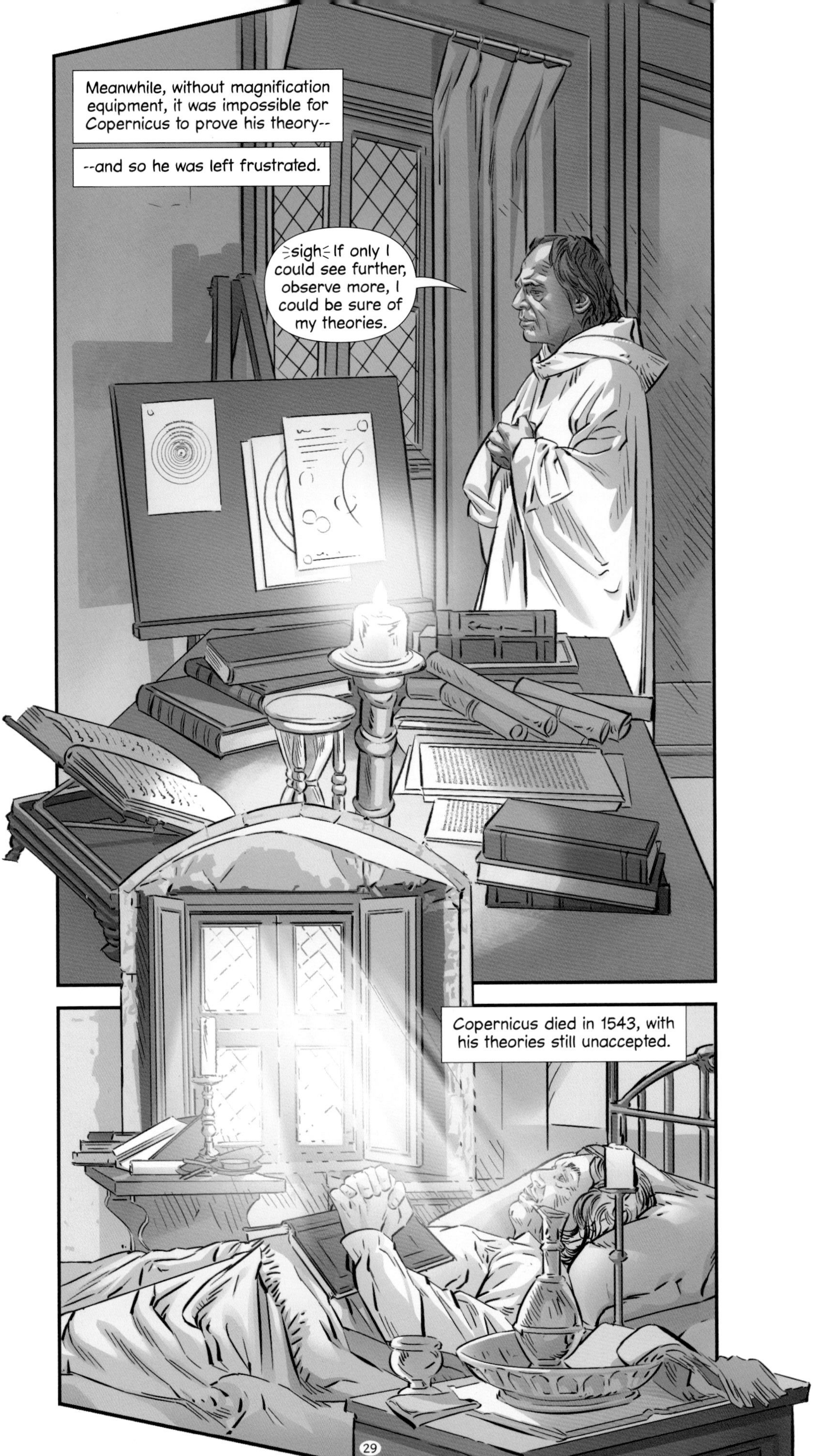
Meanwhile, without magnification equipment, it was impossible for Copernicus to prove his theory--
--and so he was left frustrated.
≥sigh≤ If only I could see further, observe more, I could be sure of my theories.
Copernicus died in 1543, with his theories still unaccepted.

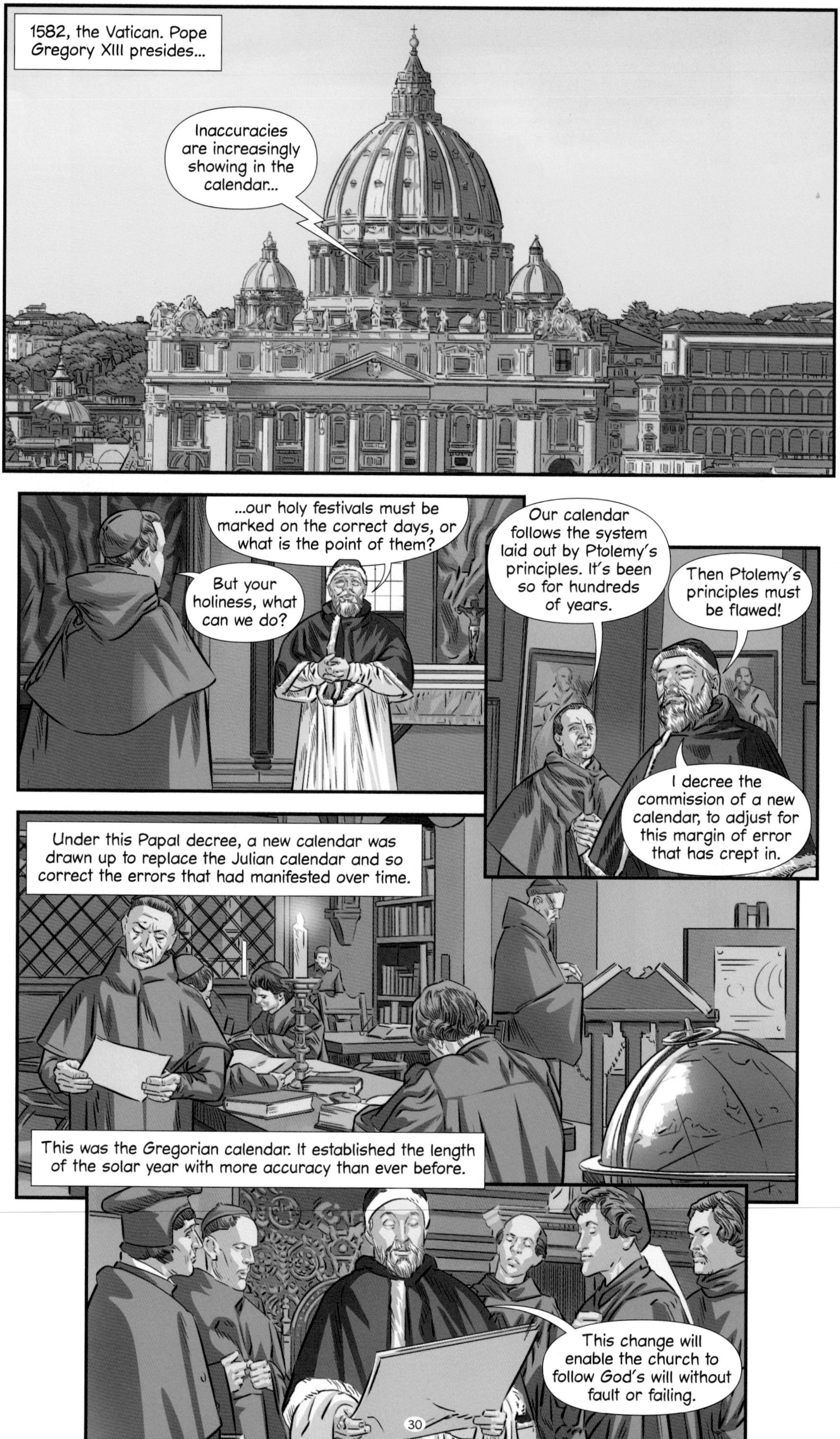

1582, the Vatican. Pope Gregory XIII presides...
Inaccuracies are increasingly showing in the calendar...
...our holy festivals must be marked on the correct days, or what is the point of them?
But your holiness, what can we do?
Our calendar follows the system laid out by Ptolemy's principles. It's been so for hundreds of years.
Then Ptolemy's principles must be flawed!
I decree the commission of a new calendar, to adjust for this margin of error that has crept in.
Under this Papal decree, a new calendar was drawn up to replace the Julian calendar and so correct the errors that had manifested over time.
This was the Gregorian calendar. It established the length of the solar year with more accuracy than ever before.
This change will enable the church to follow God's will without fault or failing.

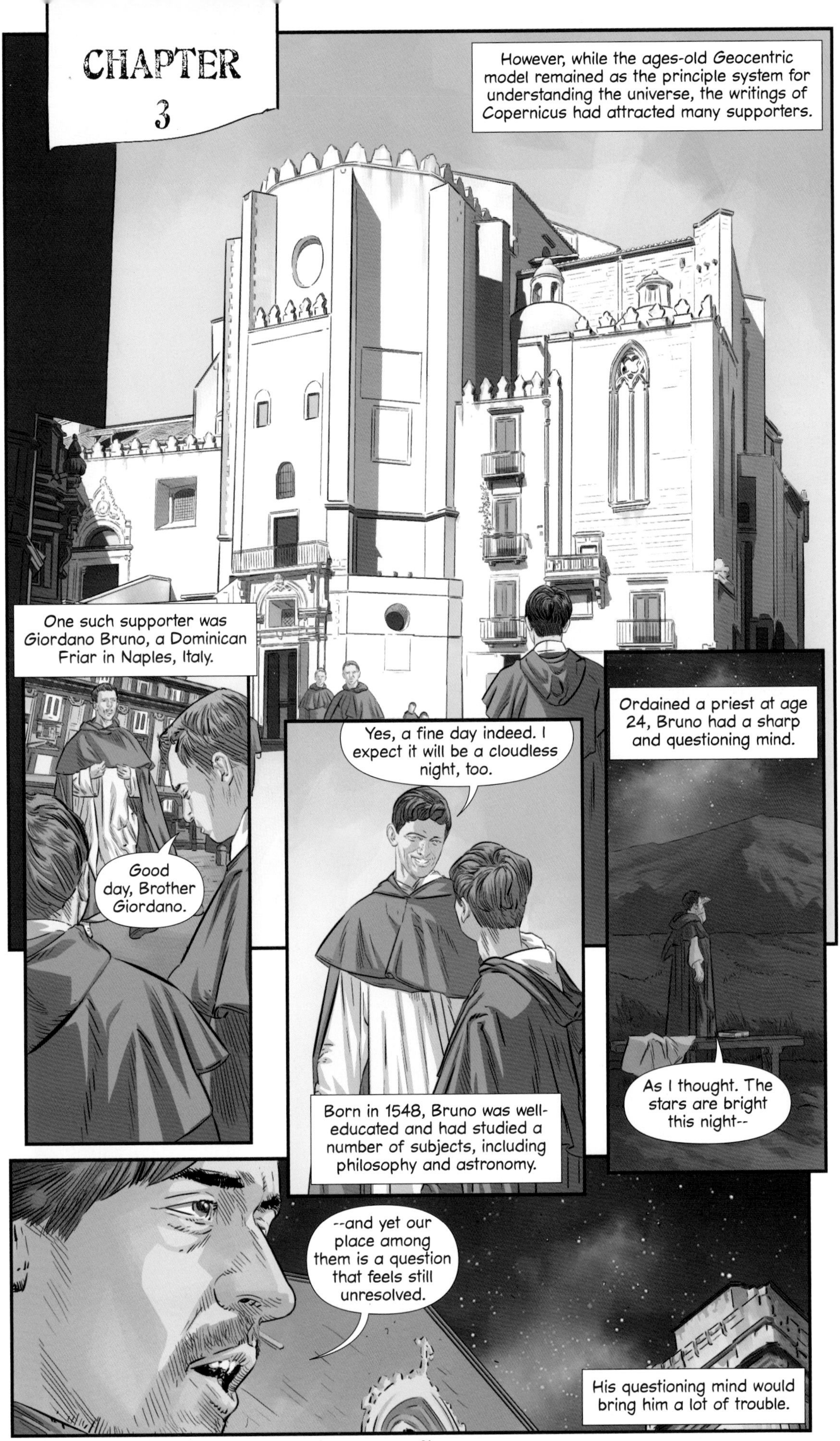
CHAPTER 3
However, while the ages-old Geocentric model remained as the principle system for understanding the universe, the writings of Copernicus had attracted many supporters.
One such supporter was Giordano Bruno, a Dominican Friar in Naples, Italy.
Good day, Brother Giordano.
Yes, a fine day indeed. I expect it will be a cloudless night, too.
Born in 1548, Bruno was well-educated and had studied a number of subjects, including philosophy and astronomy.
Ordained a priest at age 24, Bruno had a sharp and questioning mind.
As I thought. The stars are bright this night--
--and yet our place among them is a question that feels still unresolved.
His questioning mind would bring him a lot of trouble.

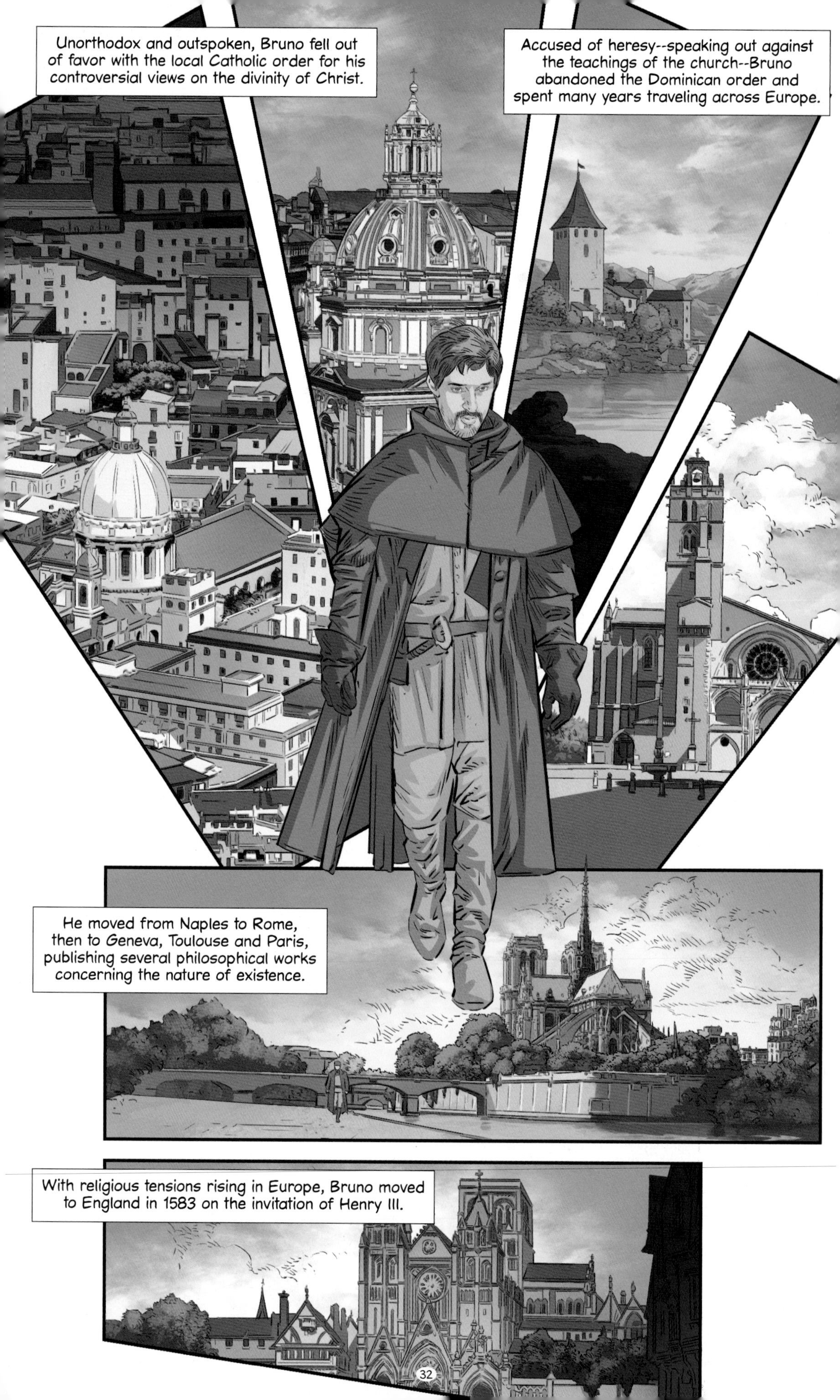
Unorthodox and outspoken, Bruno fell out of favor with the local Catholic order for his controversial views on the divinity of Christ.
Accused of heresy--speaking out against the teachings of the church--Bruno abandoned the Dominican order and spent many years traveling across Europe.
He moved from Naples to Rome, then to Geneva, Toulouse and Paris, publishing several philosophical works concerning the nature of existence.
With religious tensions rising in Europe, Bruno moved to England in 1583 on the invitation of Henry III.

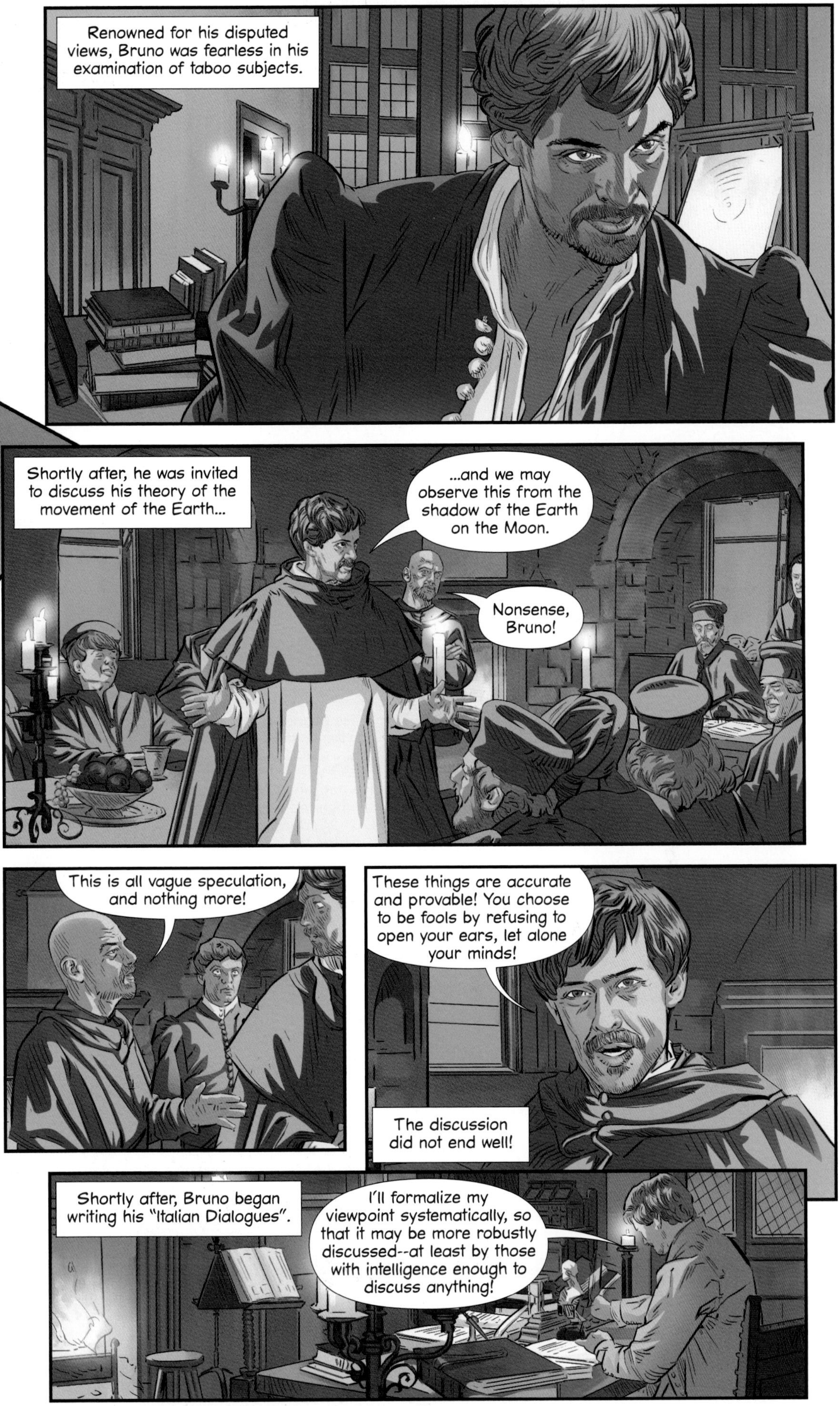
Renowned for his disputed views, Bruno was fearless in his examination of taboo subjects.
Shortly after, he was invited to discuss his theory of the movement of the Earth...
...and we may observe this from the shadow of the Earth on the Moon.
Nonsense, Bruno!
This is all vague speculation, and nothing more!
These things are accurate and provable! You choose to be fools by refusing to open your ears, let alone your minds!
The discussion did not end well!
Shortly after, Bruno began writing his "Italian Dialogues".
I'll formalize my viewpoint systematically, so that it may be more robustly discussed--at least by those with intelligence enough to discuss anything!

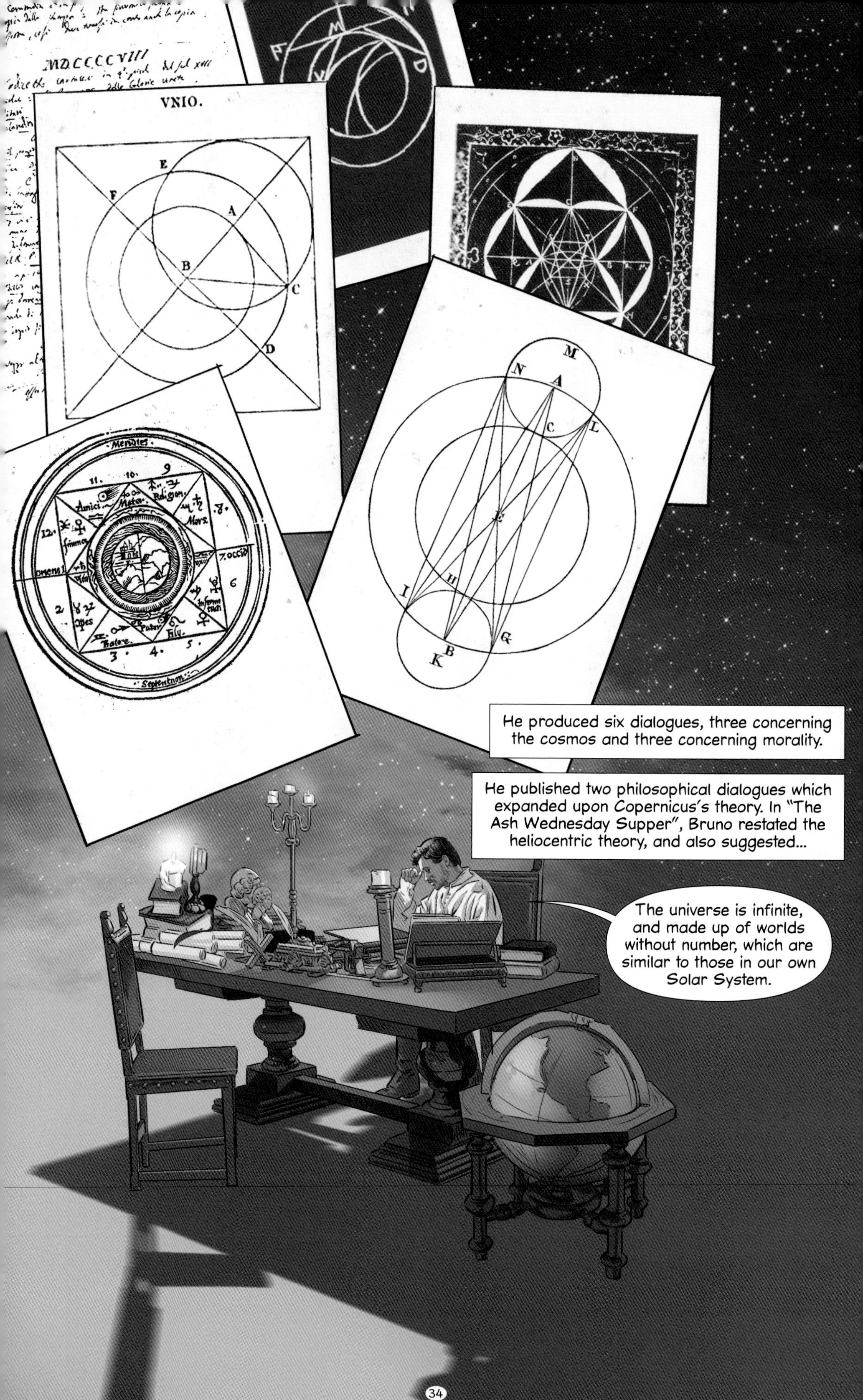
VNIO.
He produced six dialogues, three concerning the cosmos and three concerning morality.
He published two philosophical dialogues which expanded upon Copernicus's theory. In "The Ash Wednesday Supper", Bruno restated the heliocentric theory, and also suggested...
The universe is infinite, and made up of worlds without number, which are similar to those in our own Solar System.

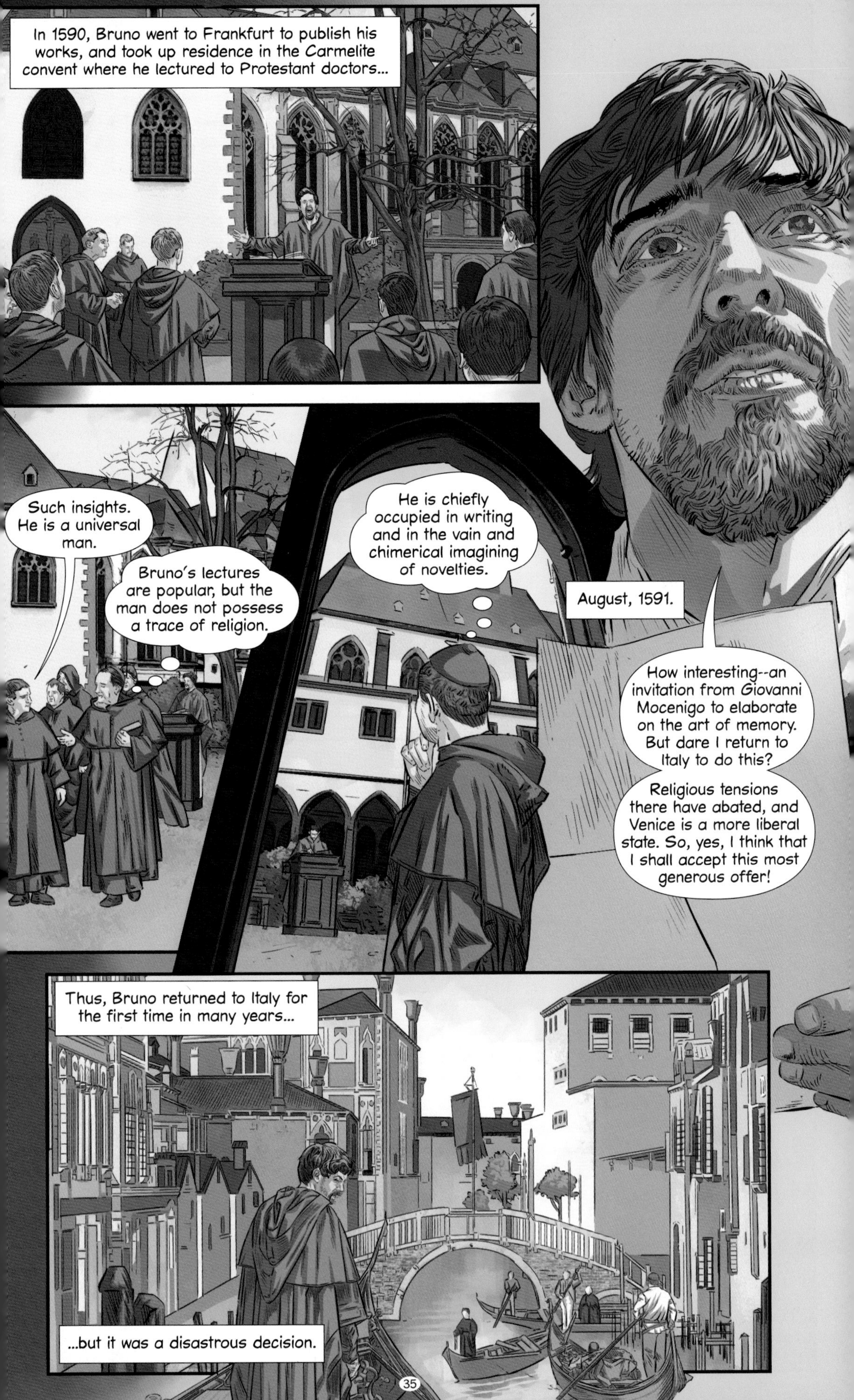
In 1590, Bruno went to Frankfurt to publish his works, and took up residence in the Carmelite convent where he lectured to Protestant doctors...
Such insights. He is a universal man.
Bruno's lectures are popular, but the man does not possess a trace of religion.
He is chiefly occupied in writing and in the vain and chimerical imagining of novelties.
August, 1591.
How interesting--an invitation from Giovanni Mocenigo to elaborate on the art of memory. But dare I return to Italy to do this?
Religious tensions there have abated, and Venice is a more liberal state. So, yes, I think that I shall accept this most generous offer!
Thus, Bruno returned to Italy for the first time in many years...
...but it was a disastrous decision.

Signore Bruno, I am so pleased that you could make it. How was your trip?

Long and tiresome, Signore Mocenigo--

--but worth it to revisit Italy after such a time away, and for such a keen student as yourself.

I hope to live up to your expectations, Signore!

Bruno taught with passion, ever fearless in challenging accepted wisdom...

Slow down! Slow down! I can barely keep up, sir!

However, by spring of the next year, Bruno longed to continue with his own academic papers, and so...

I have enjoyed teaching you, Giovanni, but I'm afraid I shall be returning to Frankfurt shortly for the publication of a new work.

That is most upsetting, Giordano.

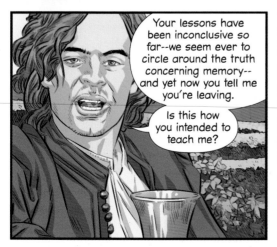

Your lessons have been inconclusive so far--we seem ever to circle around the truth concerning memory-- and yet now you tell me you're leaving.

Is this how you intended to teach me?

I can only share my ideas. I am sorry if you have found that was not enough for you, Signore Mocenigo.

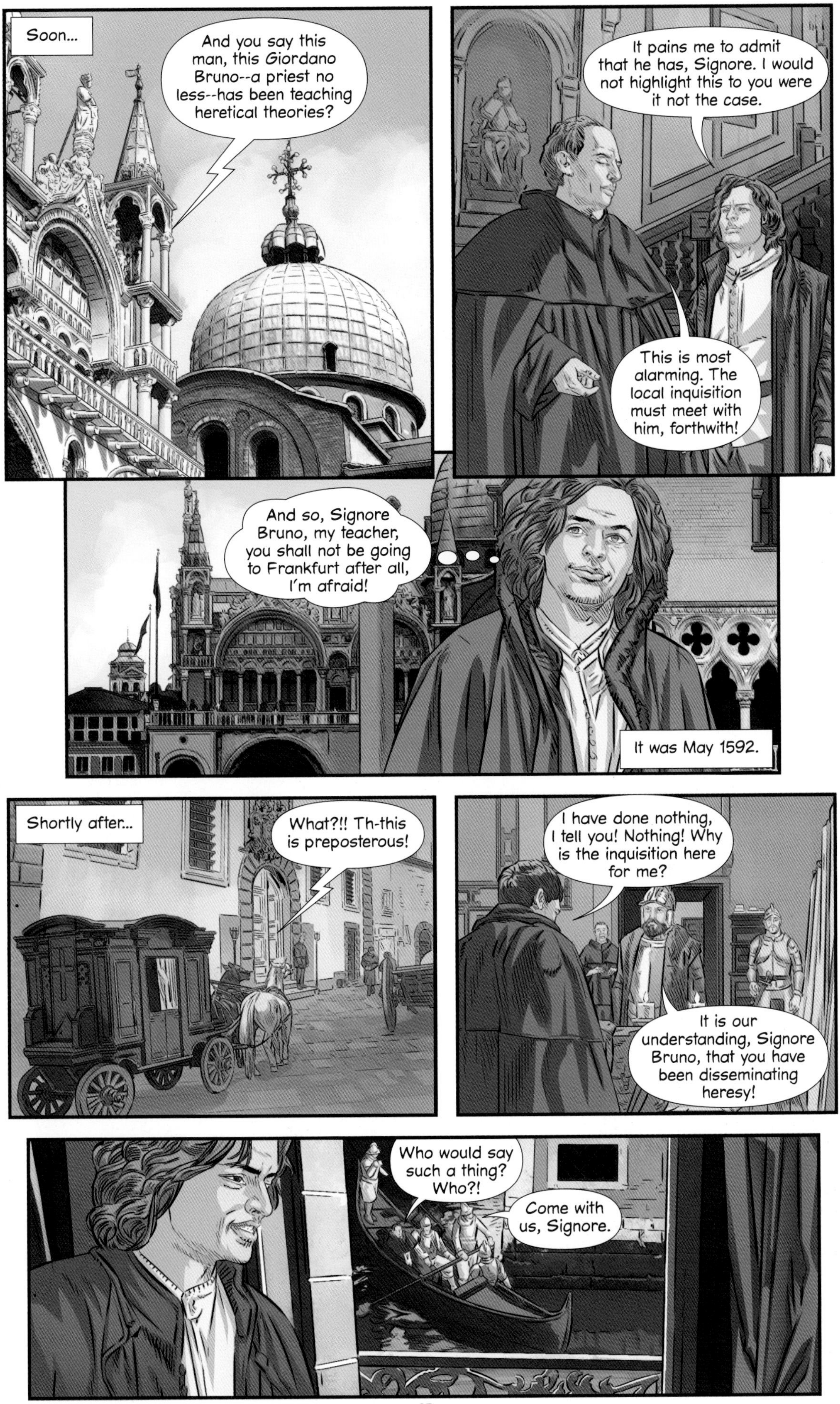
Soon...
And you say this man, this Giordano Bruno--a priest no less--has been teaching heretical theories?
It pains me to admit that he has, Signore. I would not highlight this to you were it not the case.
This is most alarming. The local inquisition must meet with him, forthwith!
And so, Signore Bruno, my teacher, you shall not be going to Frankfurt after all, I'm afraid!
It was May 1592.
Shortly after...
What?!! Th-this is preposterous!
I have done nothing, I tell you! Nothing! Why is the inquisition here for me?
It is our understanding, Signore Bruno, that you have been disseminating heresy!
Who would say such a thing? Who?!
Come with us, Signore.

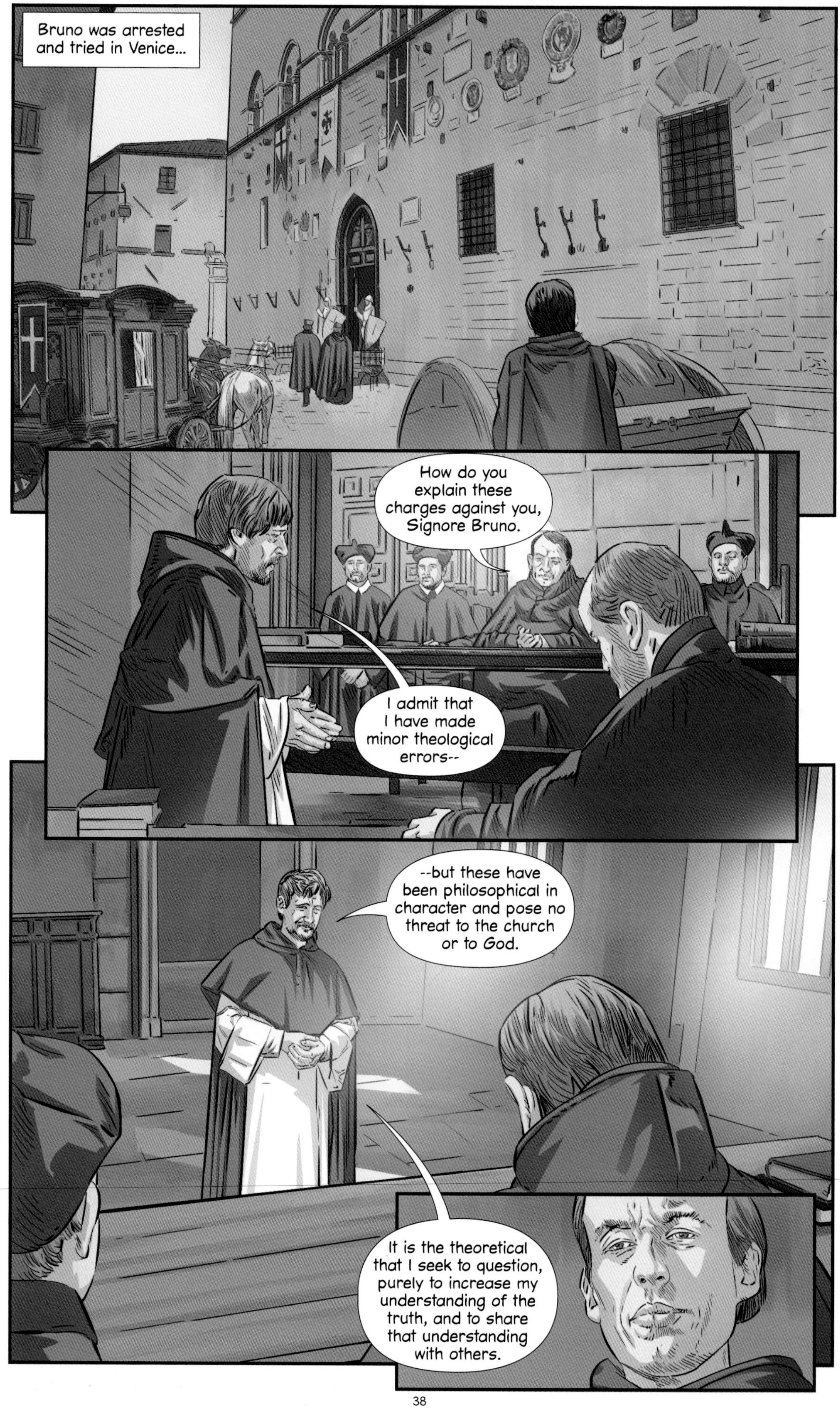
Bruno was arrested and tried in Venice...
How do you explain these charges against you, Signore Bruno.
I admit that I have made minor theological errors--
--but these have been philosophical in character and pose no threat to the church or to God.
It is the theoretical that I seek to question, purely to increase my understanding of the truth, and to share that understanding with others.

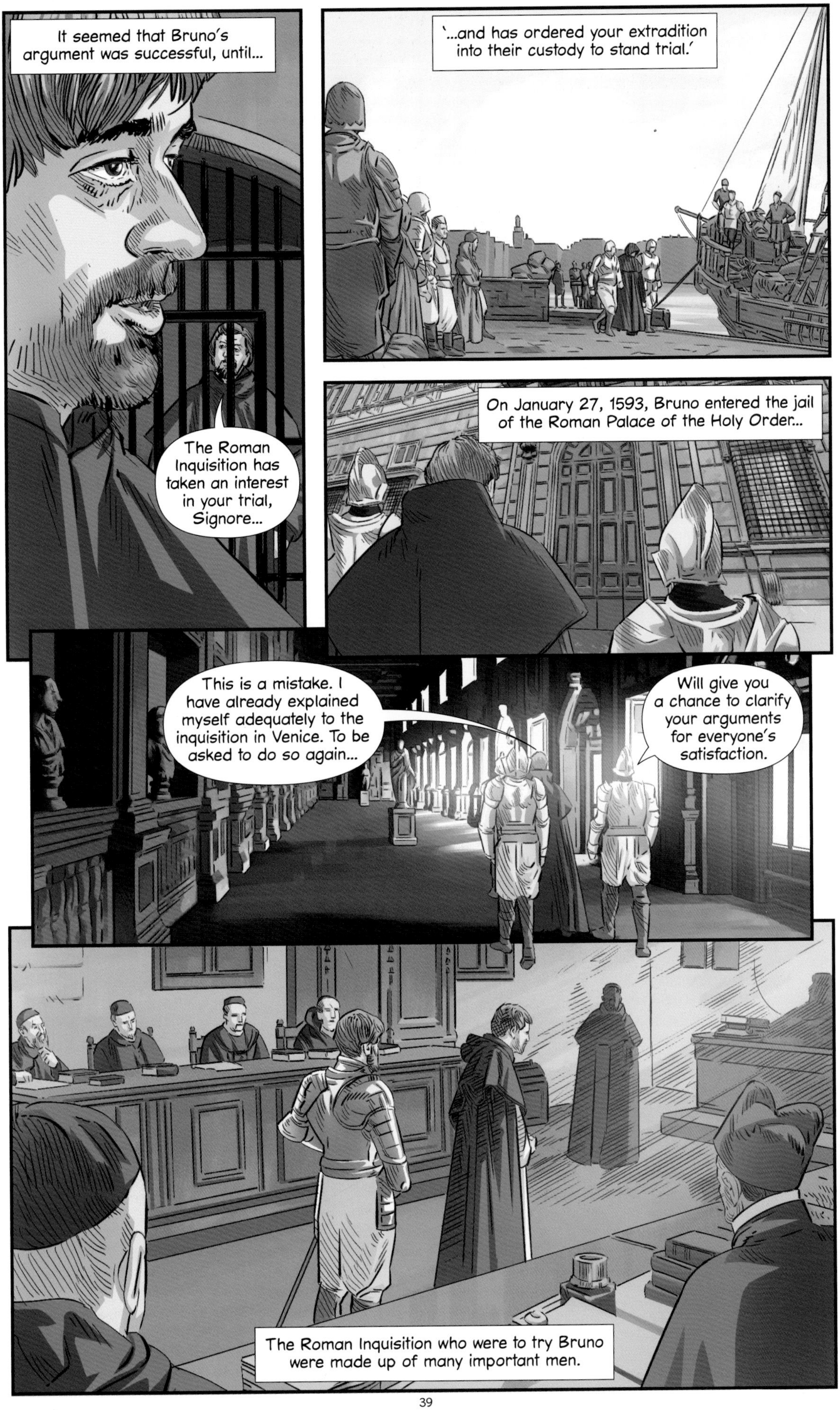
It seemed that Bruno's argument was successful, until...
The Roman Inquisition has taken an interest in your trial, Signore...
'...and has ordered your extradition into their custody to stand trial.'
On January 27, 1593, Bruno entered the jail of the Roman Palace of the Holy Order...
This is a mistake. I have already explained myself adequately to the inquisition in Venice. To be asked to do so again...
Will give you a chance to clarify your arguments for everyone's satisfaction.
The Roman Inquisition who were to try Bruno were made up of many important men.

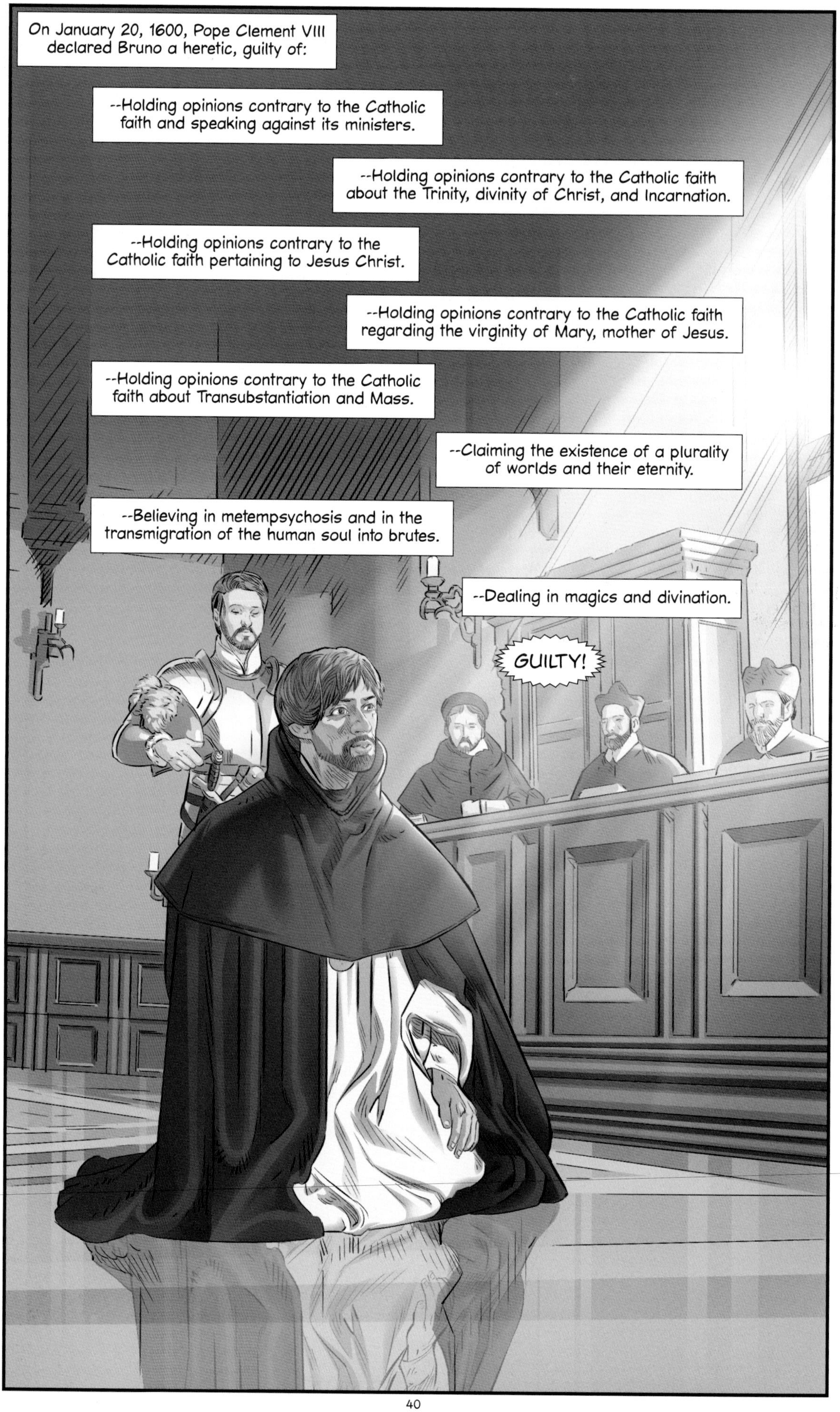
On January 20, 1600, Pope Clement VIII declared Bruno a heretic, guilty of:
--Holding opinions contrary to the Catholic faith and speaking against its ministers.
--Holding opinions contrary to the Catholic faith about the Trinity, divinity of Christ, and Incarnation.
--Holding opinions contrary to the Catholic faith pertaining to Jesus Christ.
--Holding opinions contrary to the Catholic faith regarding the virginity of Mary, mother of Jesus.
--Holding opinions contrary to the Catholic faith about Transubstantiation and Mass.
--Claiming the existence of a plurality of worlds and their eternity.
--Believing in metempsychosis and in the transmigration of the human soul into brutes.
--Dealing in magics and divination.
GUILTY!

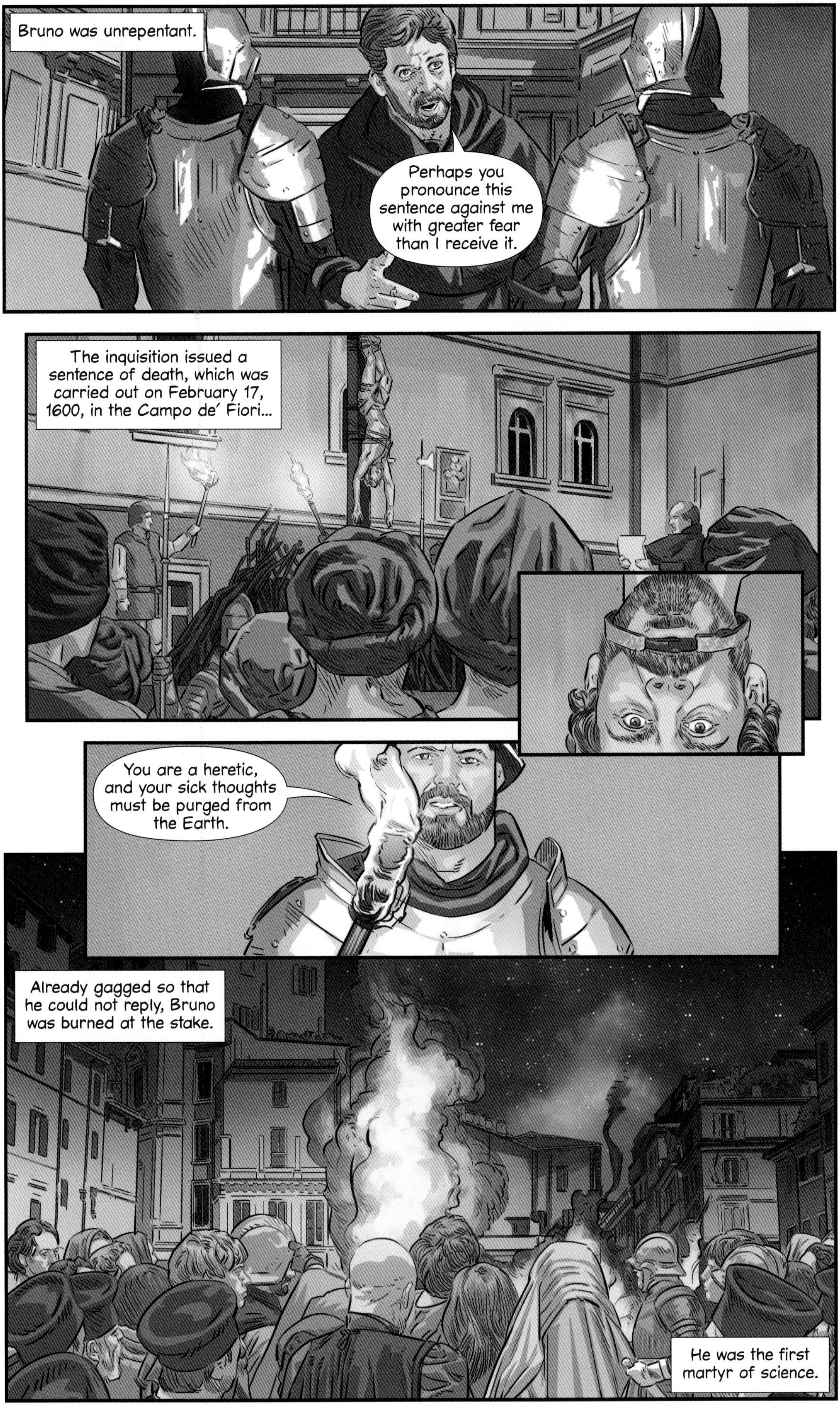

Bruno was unrepentant.
Perhaps you pronounce this sentence against me with greater fear than I receive it.
The inquisition issued a sentence of death, which was carried out on February 17, 1600, in the Campo de' Fiori...
You are a heretic, and your sick thoughts must be purged from the Earth.
Already gagged so that he could not reply, Bruno was burned at the stake.
He was the first martyr of science.

CHAPTER 4

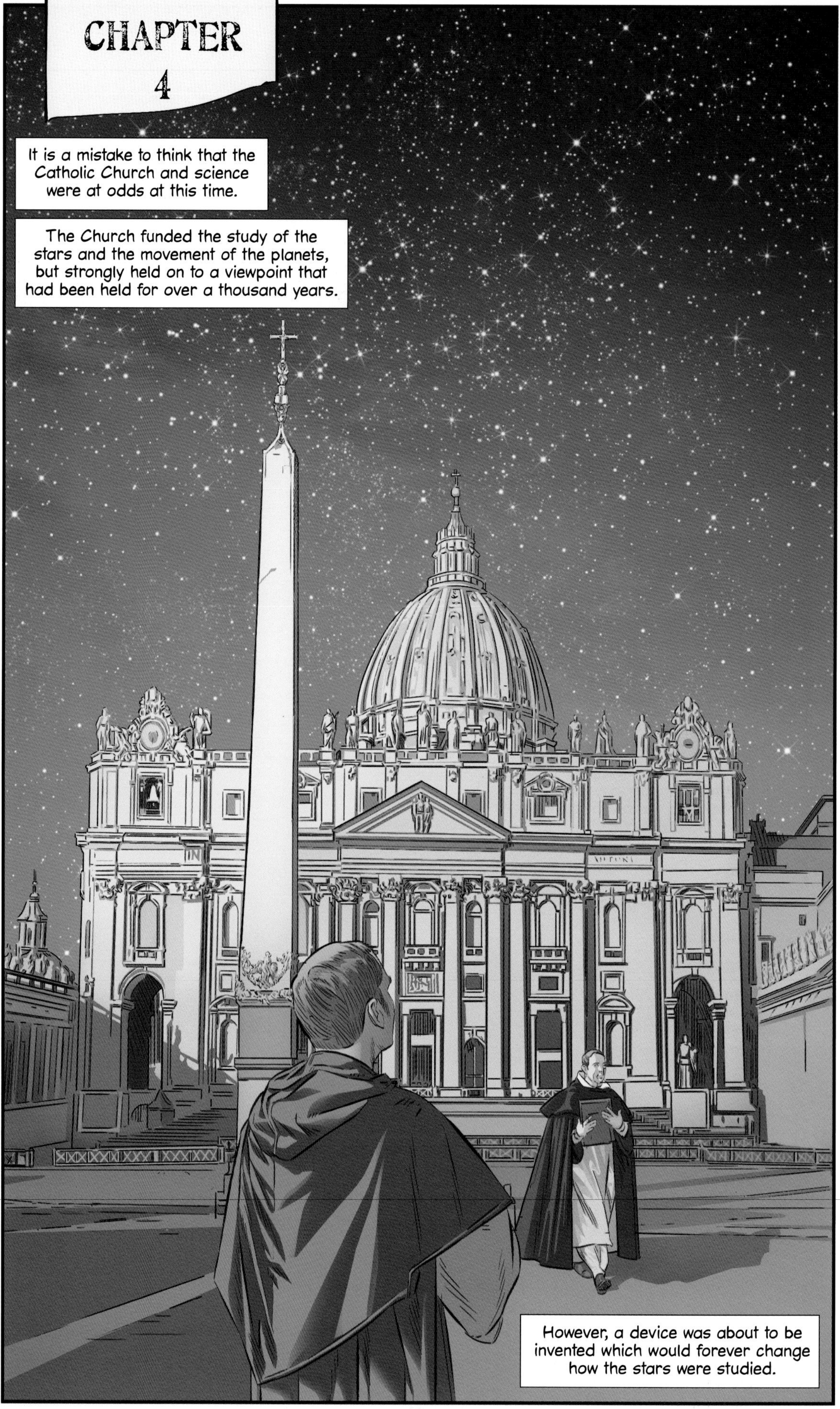
It is a mistake to think that the Catholic Church and science were at odds at this time.
The Church funded the study of the stars and the movement of the planets, but strongly held on to a viewpoint that had been held for over a thousand years.
However, a device was about to be invented which would forever change how the stars were studied.

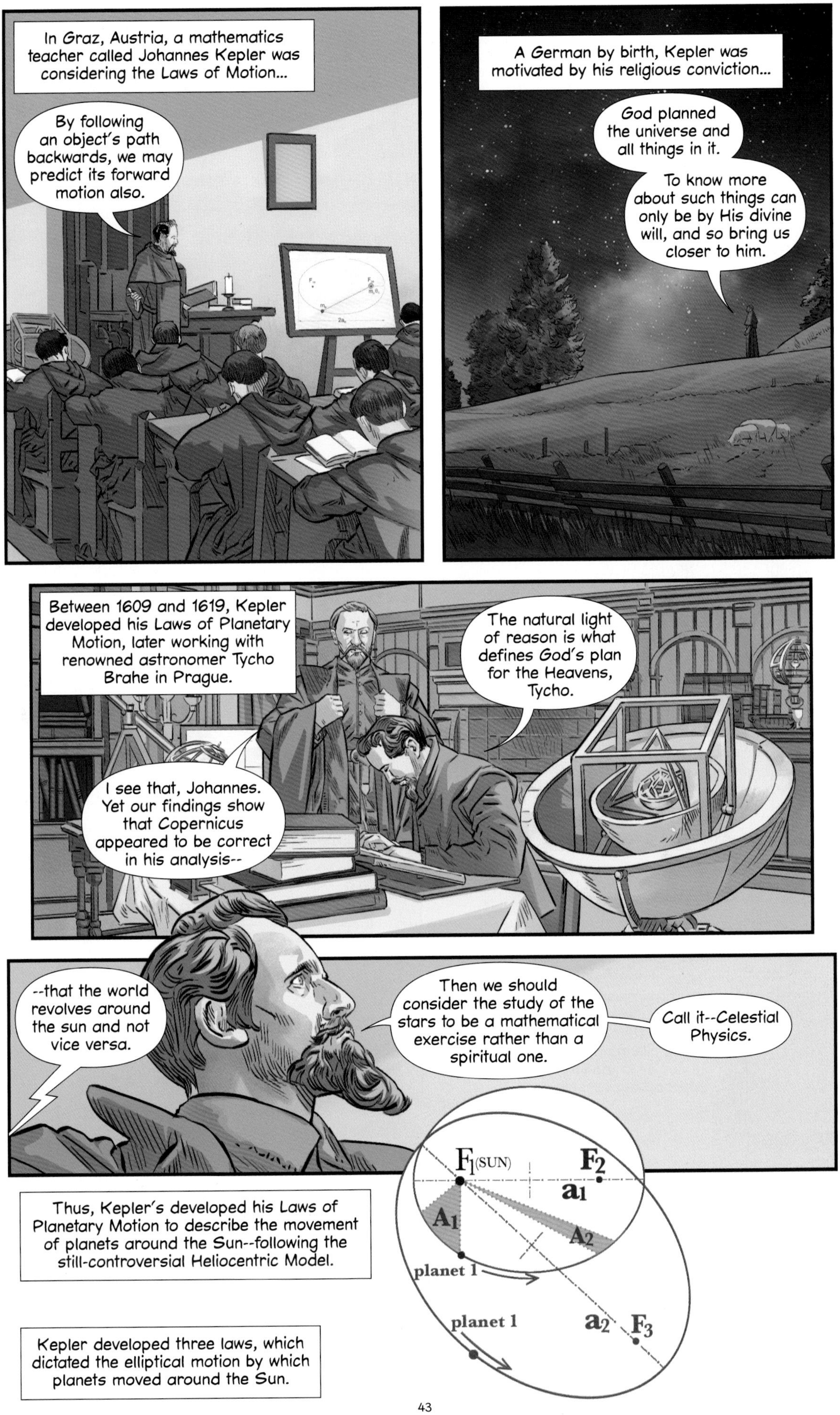
In Graz, Austria, a mathematics teacher called Johannes Kepler was considering the Laws of Motion...
By following an object's path backwards, we may predict its forward motion also.
A German by birth, Kepler was motivated by his religious conviction...
God planned the universe and all things in it.
To know more about such things can only be by His divine will, and so bring us closer to him.
Between 1609 and 1619, Kepler developed his Laws of Planetary Motion, later working with renowned astronomer Tycho Brahe in Prague.
The natural light of reason is what defines God's plan for the Heavens, Tycho.
I see that, Johannes. Yet our findings show that Copernicus appeared to be correct in his analysis--
--that the world revolves around the sun and not vice versa.
Then we should consider the study of the stars to be a mathematical exercise rather than a spiritual one.
Call it--Celestial Physics.
Thus, Kepler's developed his Laws of Planetary Motion to describe the movement of planets around the Sun--following the still-controversial Heliocentric Model.
Kepler developed three laws, which dictated the elliptical motion by which planets moved around the Sun.
F1 (SUN)
F2
a1
A1
A2
planet 1
planet 1
a2
F3

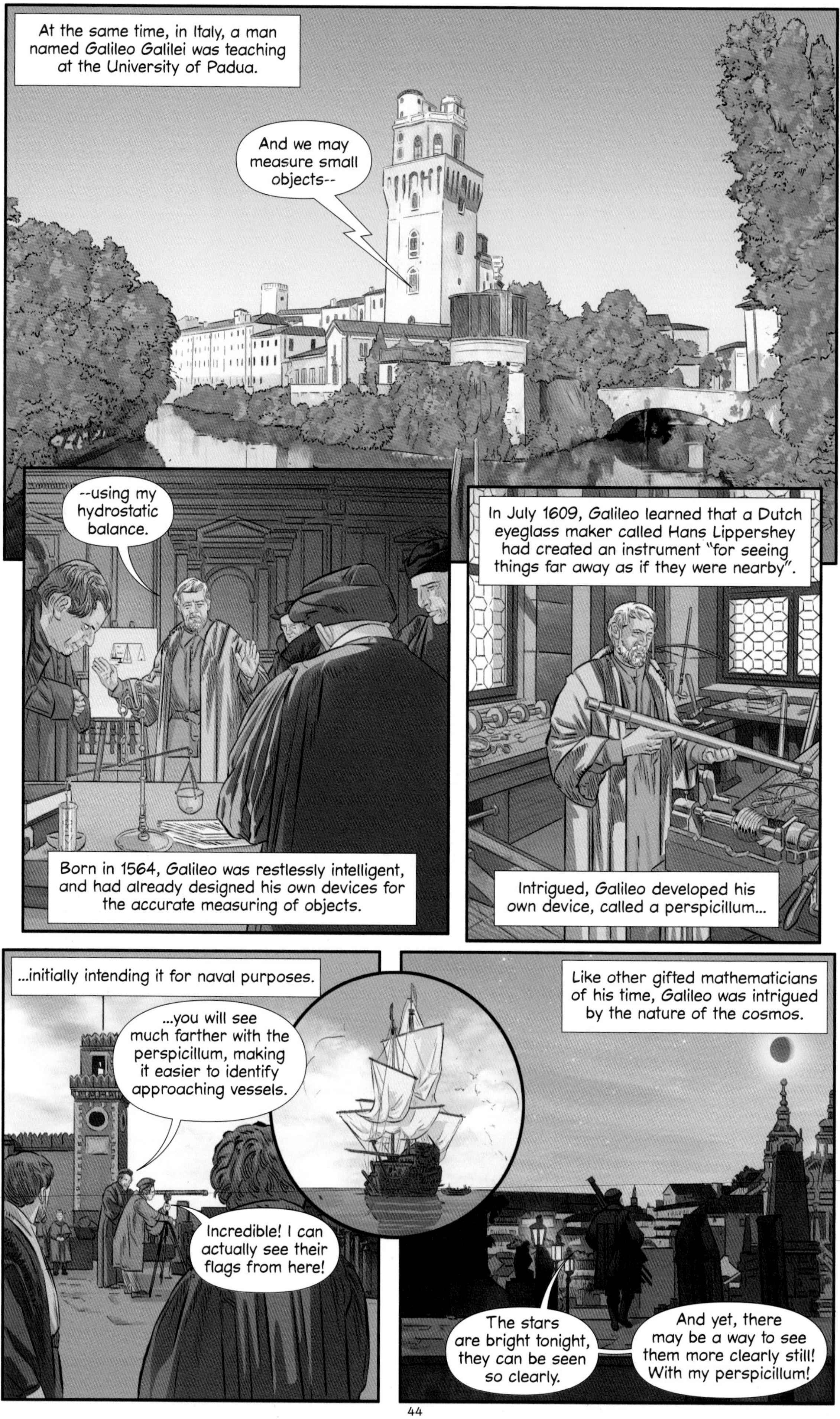
At the same time, in Italy, a man named Galileo Galilei was teaching at the University of Padua.
And we may measure small objects--
--using my hydrostatic balance.
Born in 1564, Galileo was restlessly intelligent, and had already designed his own devices for the accurate measuring of objects.
In July 1609, Galileo learned that a Dutch eyeglass maker called Hans Lippershey had created an instrument "for seeing things far away as if they were nearby".
Intrigued, Galileo developed his own device, called a perspicillum...
...initially intending it for naval purposes.
...you will see much farther with the perspicillum, making it easier to identify approaching vessels.
Incredible! I can actually see their flags from here!
Like other gifted mathematicians of his time, Galileo was intrigued by the nature of the cosmos.
The stars are bright tonight, they can be seen so clearly.
And yet, there may be a way to see them more clearly still! With my perspicillum!

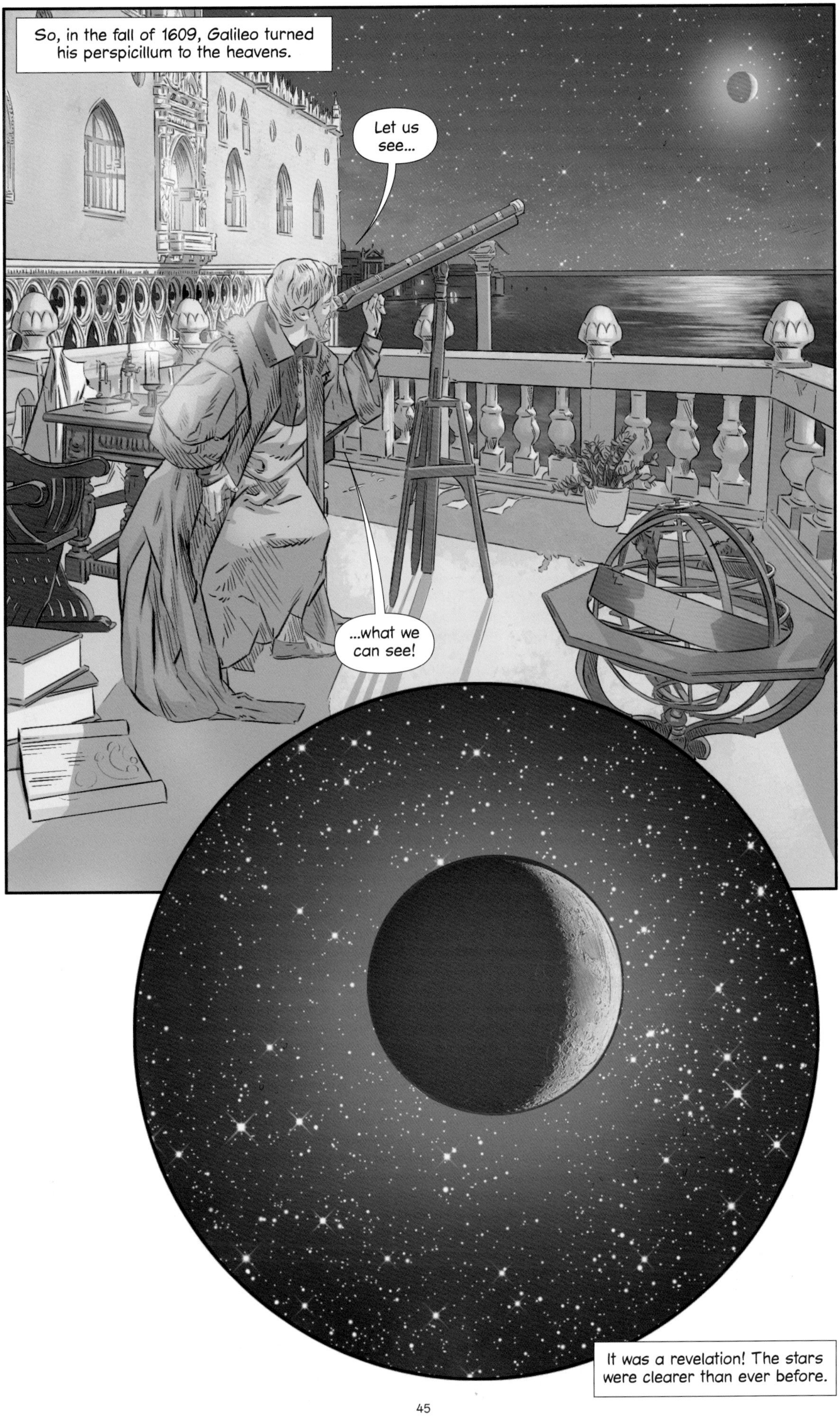
So, in the fall of 1609, Galileo turned his perspicillum to the heavens.
Let us see...
...what we can see!
It was a revelation! The stars were clearer than ever before.

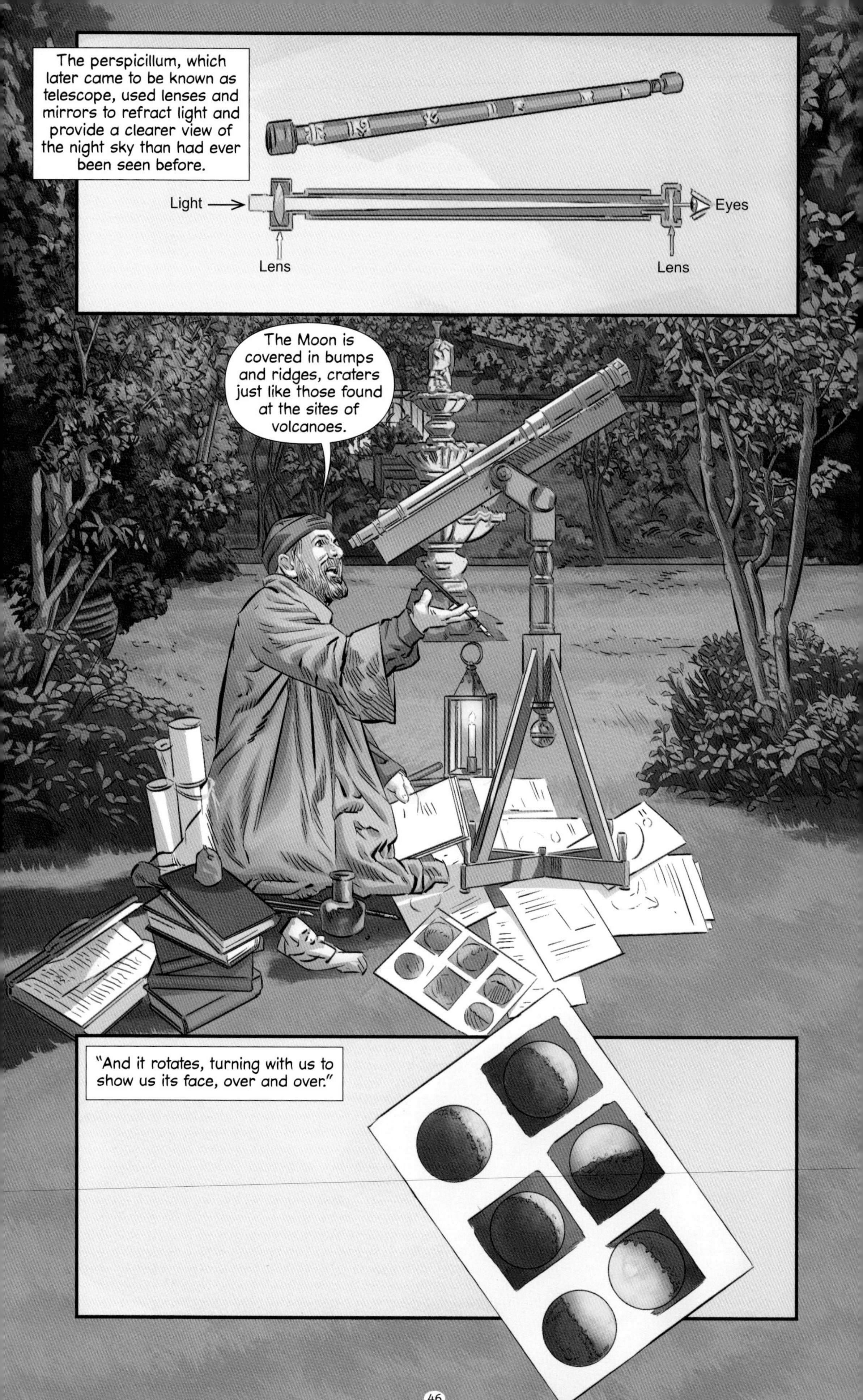
The perspicillum, which later came to be known as telescope, used lenses and mirrors to refract light and provide a clearer view of the night sky than had ever been seen before.
Light
Eyes
Lens
Lens
The Moon is covered in bumps and ridges, craters just like those found at the sites of volcanoes.
"And it rotates, turning with us to show us its face, over and over."

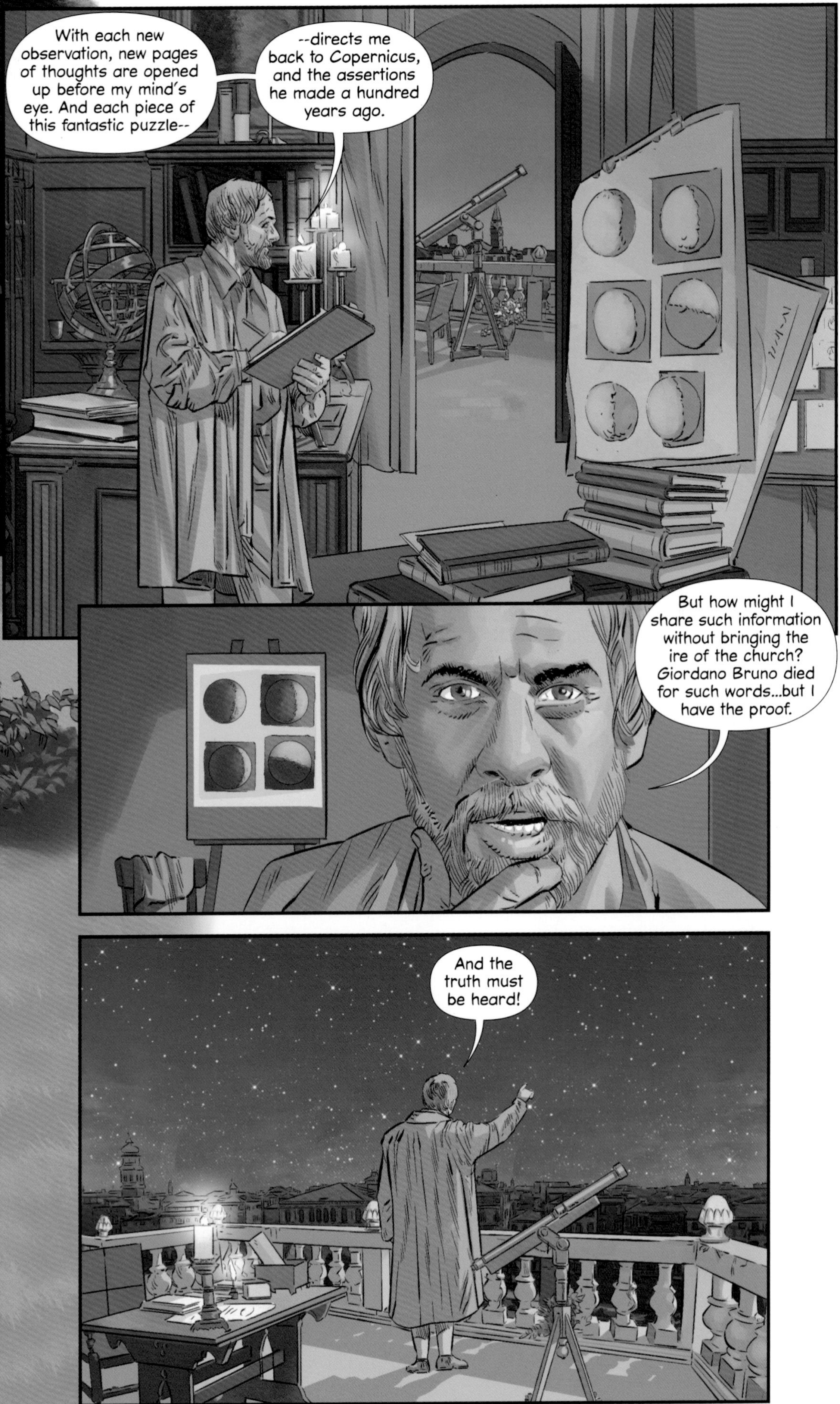
With each new observation, new pages of thoughts are opened up before my mind's eye. And each piece of this fantastic puzzle--
--directs me back to Copernicus, and the assertions he made a hundred years ago.
But how might I share such information without bringing the ire of the church? Giordano Bruno died for such words...but I have the proof.
And the truth must be heard!

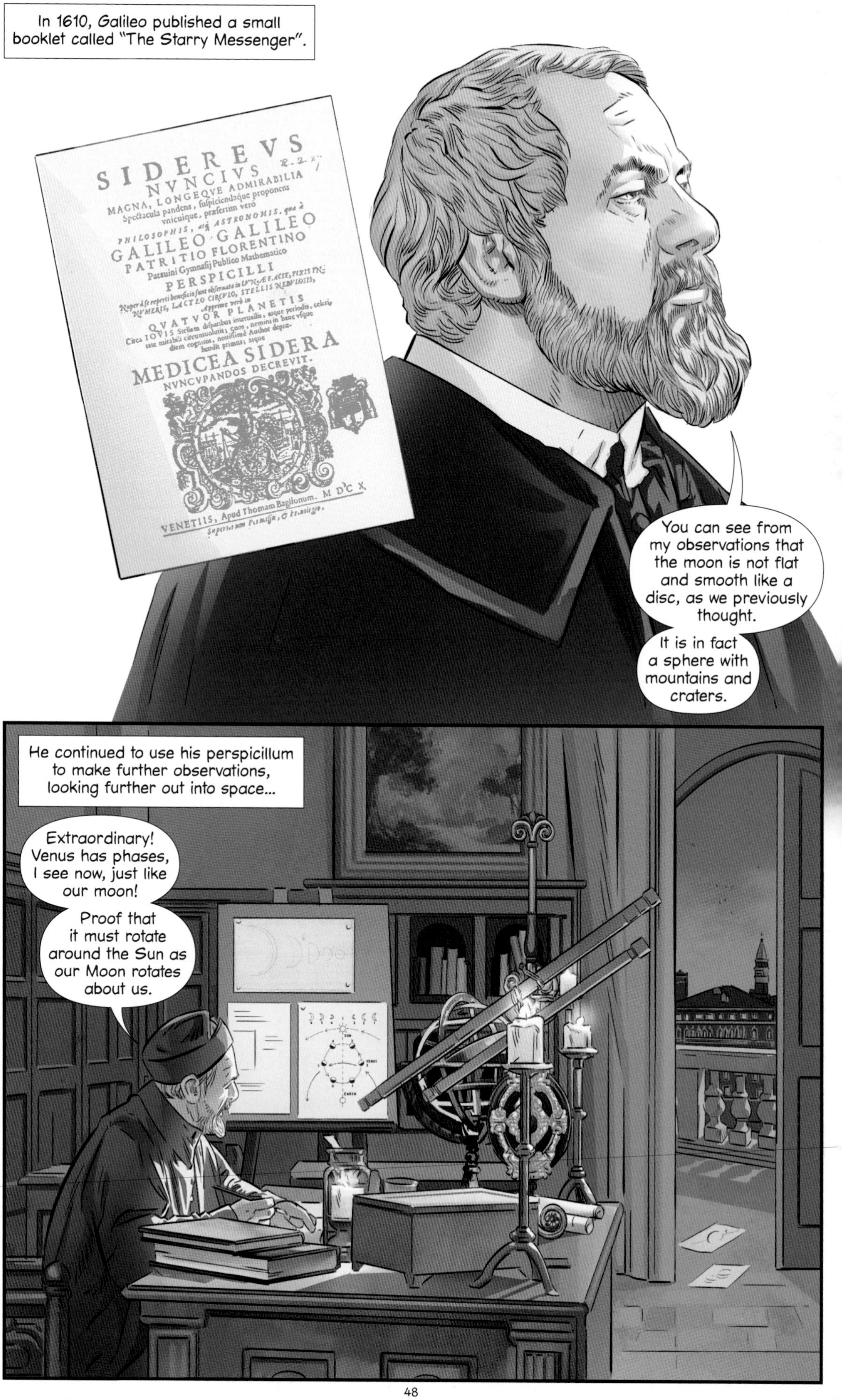
In 1610, Galileo published a small booklet called "The Starry Messenger".
SIDEREVS
NVNCIVS
GALILEO GALILEO
PATRITIO FLORENTINO
PERSPICILLI
QVATVOR PLANETIS
MEDICEA SIDERA
NVNCVPANDOS DECREVIT.
You can see from my observations that the moon is not flat and smooth like a disc, as we previously thought.
It is in fact a sphere with mountains and craters.
He continued to use his perspicillum to make further observations, looking further out into space...
Extraordinary! Venus has phases, I see now, just like our moon!
Proof that it must rotate around the Sun as our Moon rotates about us.

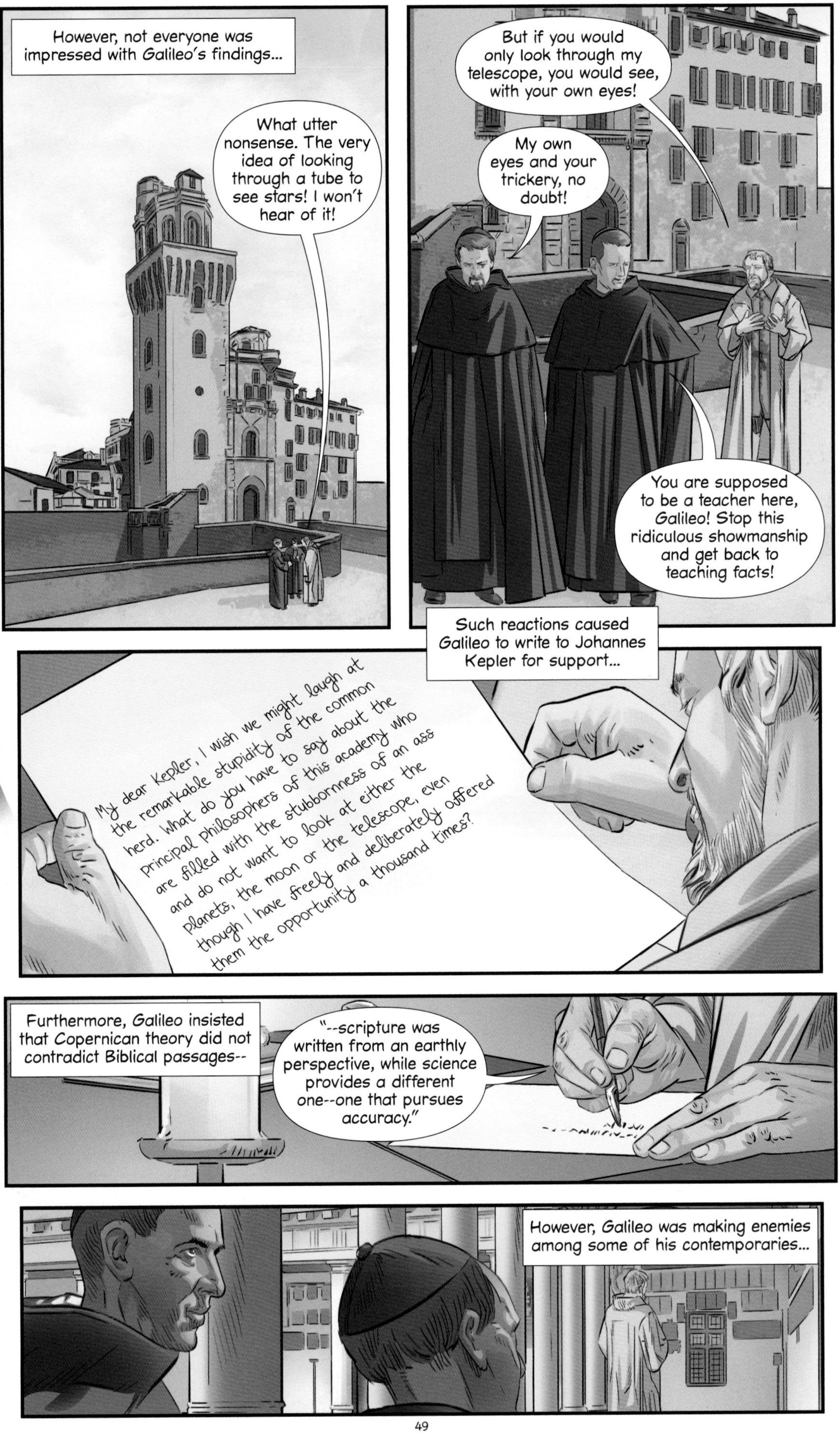
However, not everyone was impressed with Galileo's findings...
What utter nonsense. The very idea of looking through a tube to see stars! I won't hear of it!
But if you would only look through my telescope, you would see, with your own eyes!
My own eyes and your trickery, no doubt!
You are supposed to be a teacher here, Galileo! Stop this ridiculous showmanship and get back to teaching facts!
Such reactions caused Galileo to write to Johannes Kepler for support...
My dear Kepler, I wish we might laugh at
the remarkable stupidity of the common
herd. What do you have to say about the
principal philosophers of this academy who
are filled with the stubbornness of an ass
and do not want to look at either the
planets, the moon or the telescope, even
though I have freely and deliberately offered
them the opportunity a thousand times?
Furthermore, Galileo insisted that Copernican theory did not contradict Biblical passages--
"--scripture was written from an earthly perspective, while science provides a different one--one that pursues accuracy."
However, Galileo was making enemies among some of his contemporaries...

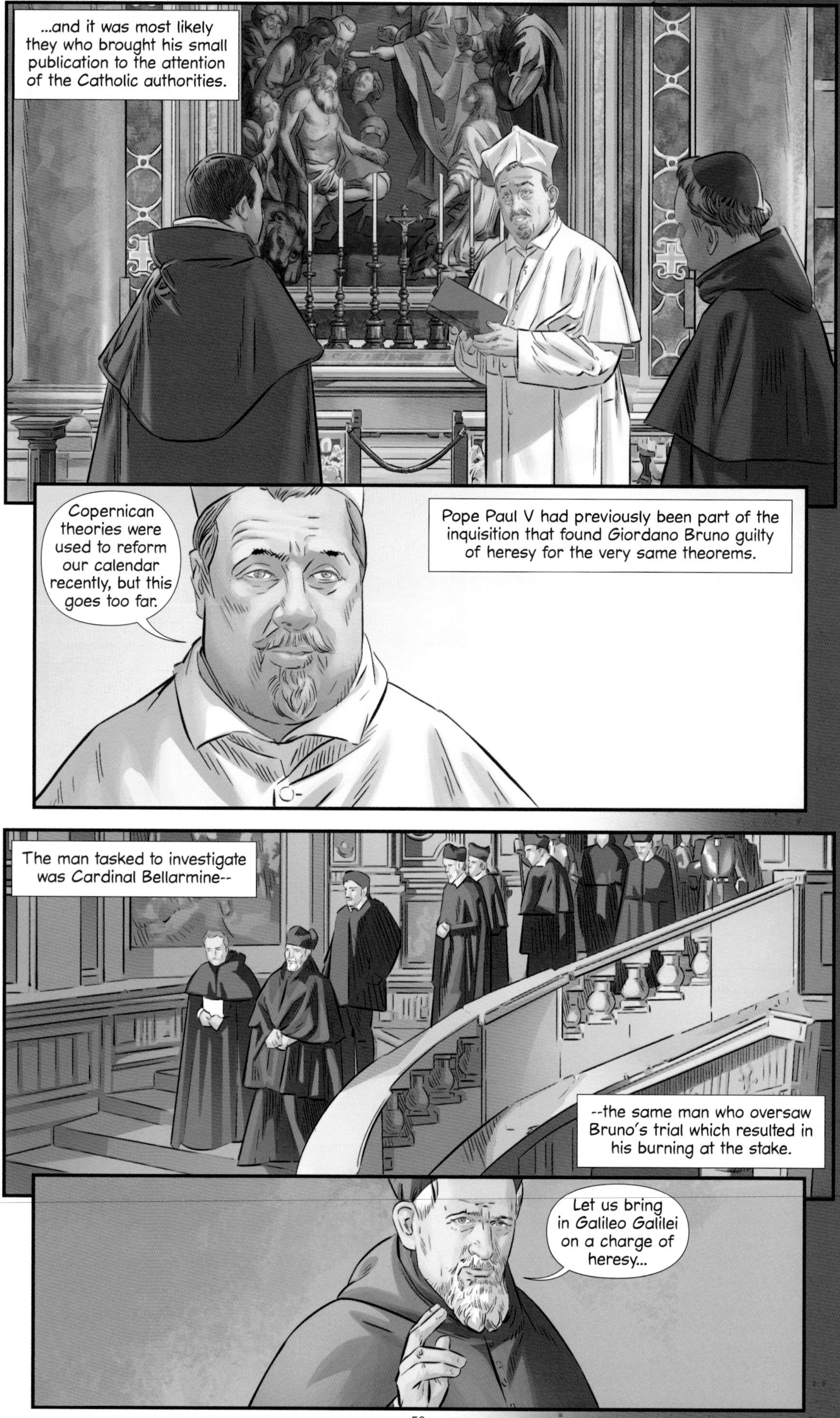
...and it was most likely they who brought his small publication to the attention of the Catholic authorities.
Copernican theories were used to reform our calendar recently, but this goes too far.
Pope Paul V had previously been part of the inquisition that found Giordano Bruno guilty of heresy for the very same theorems.
The man tasked to investigate was Cardinal Bellarmine--
--the same man who oversaw Bruno's trial which resulted in his burning at the stake.
Let us bring in Galileo Galilei on a charge of heresy...

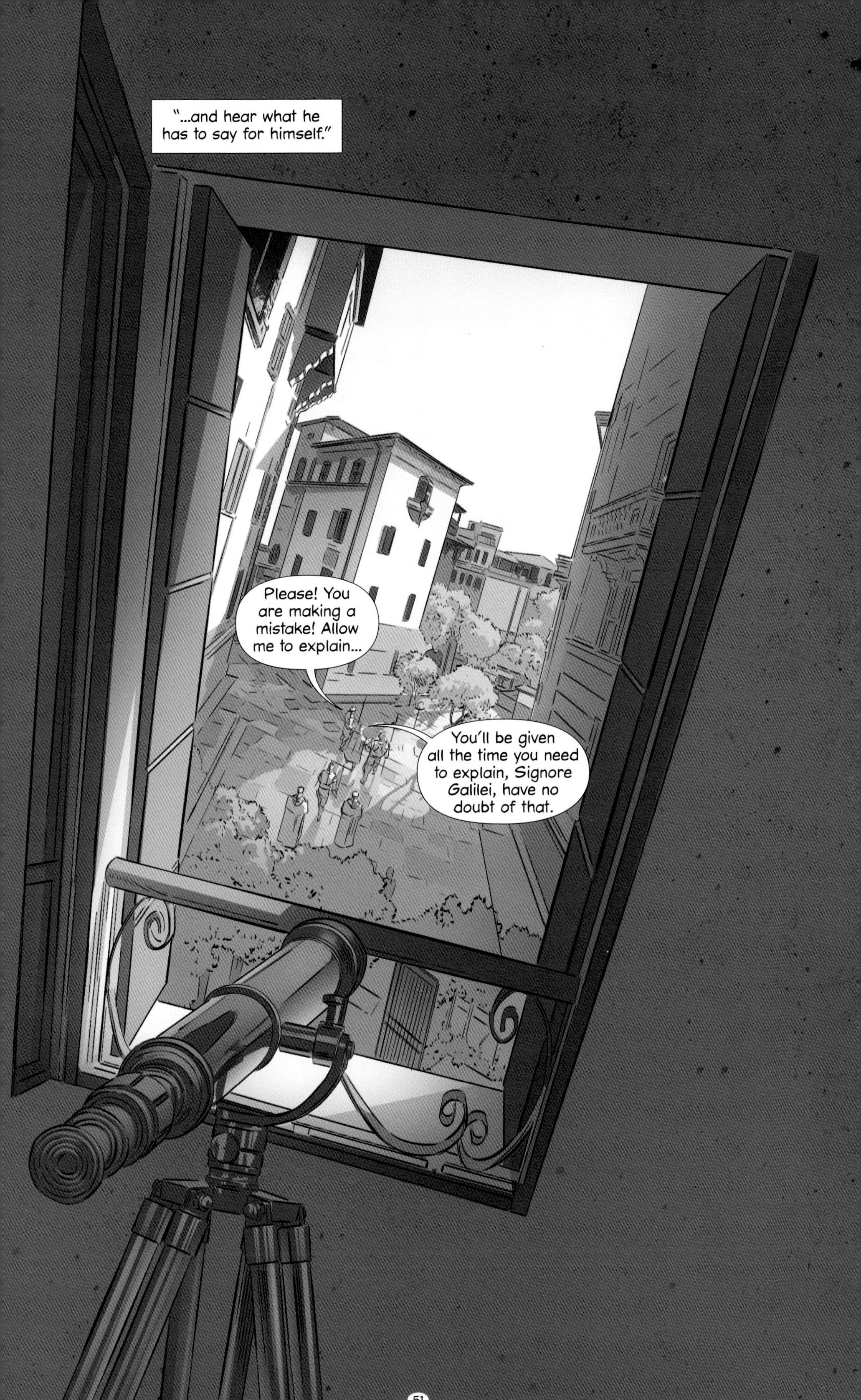
"...and hear what he has to say for himself."
Please! You are making a mistake! Allow me to explain...
You'll be given all the time you need to explain, Signore Galilei, have no doubt of that.

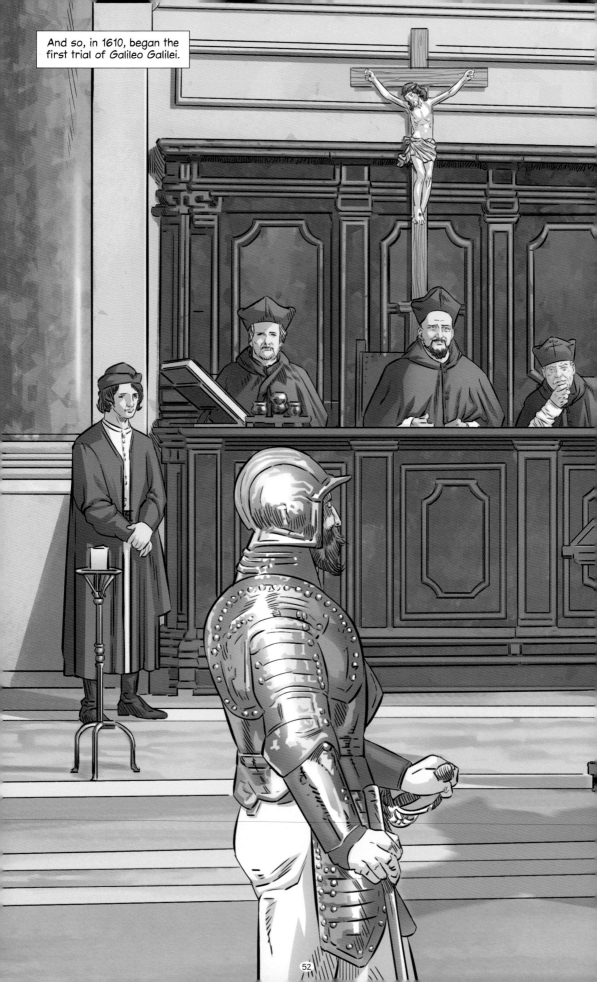

And so, in 1610, began the first trial of Galileo Galilei.

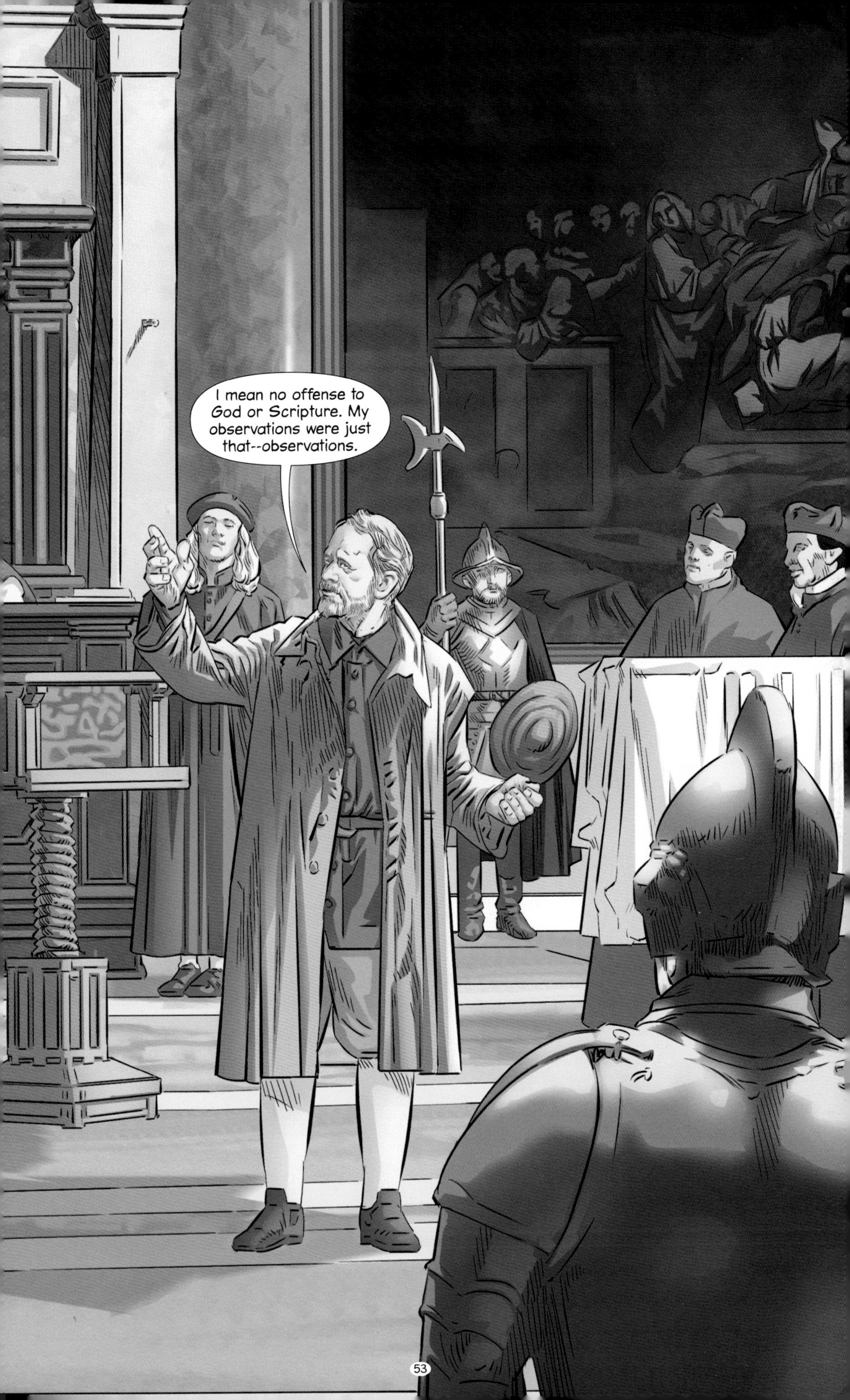
I mean no offense to God or Scripture. My observations were just that--observations.

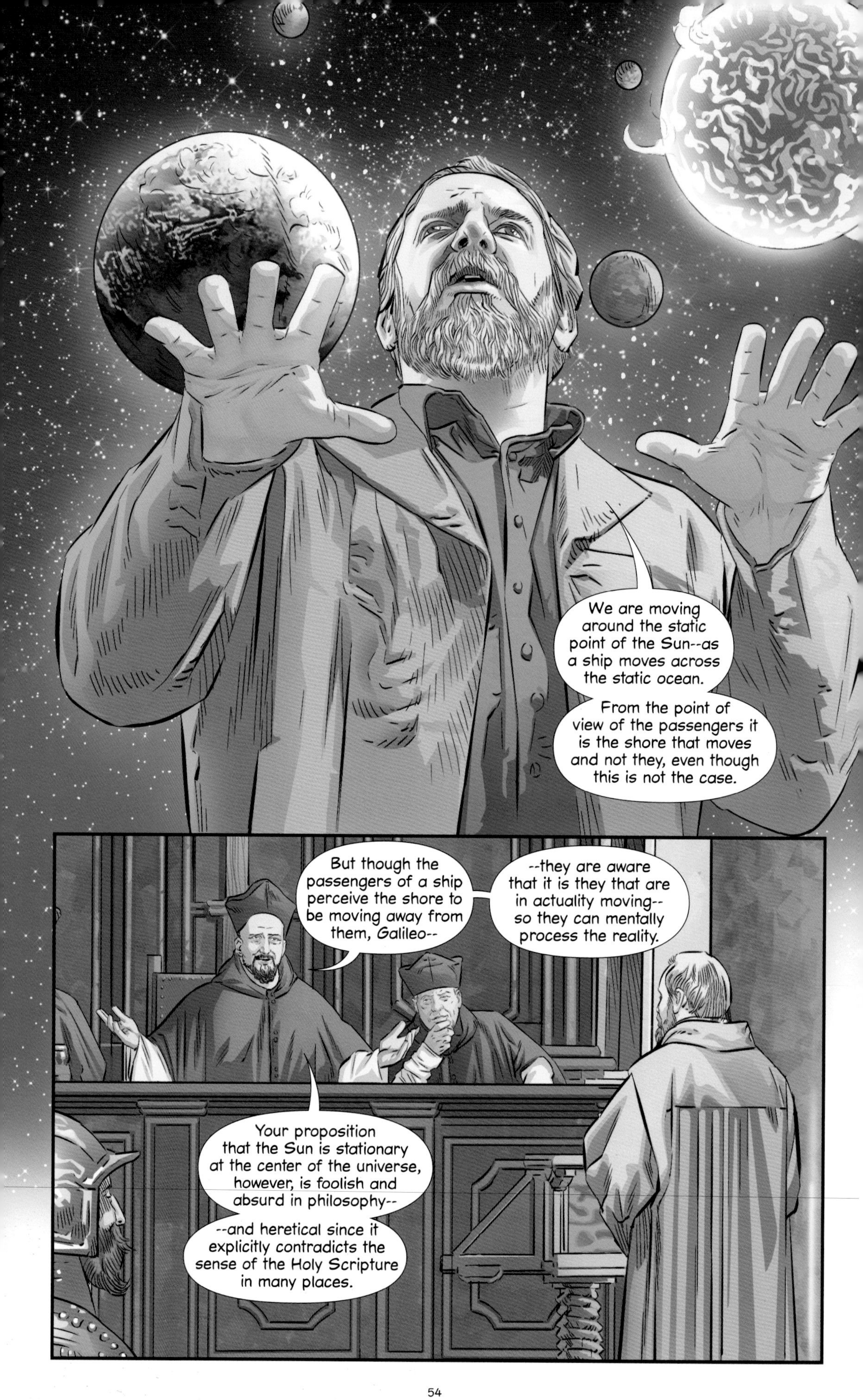
We are moving around the static point of the Sun--as a ship moves across the static ocean.
From the point of view of the passengers it is the shore that moves and not they, even though this is not the case.
But though the passengers of a ship perceive the shore to be moving away from them, Galileo--
--they are aware that it is they that are in actuality moving--so they can mentally process the reality.
Your proposition that the Sun is stationary at the center of the universe, however, is foolish and absurd in philosophy--
--and heretical since it explicitly contradicts the sense of the Holy Scripture in many places.

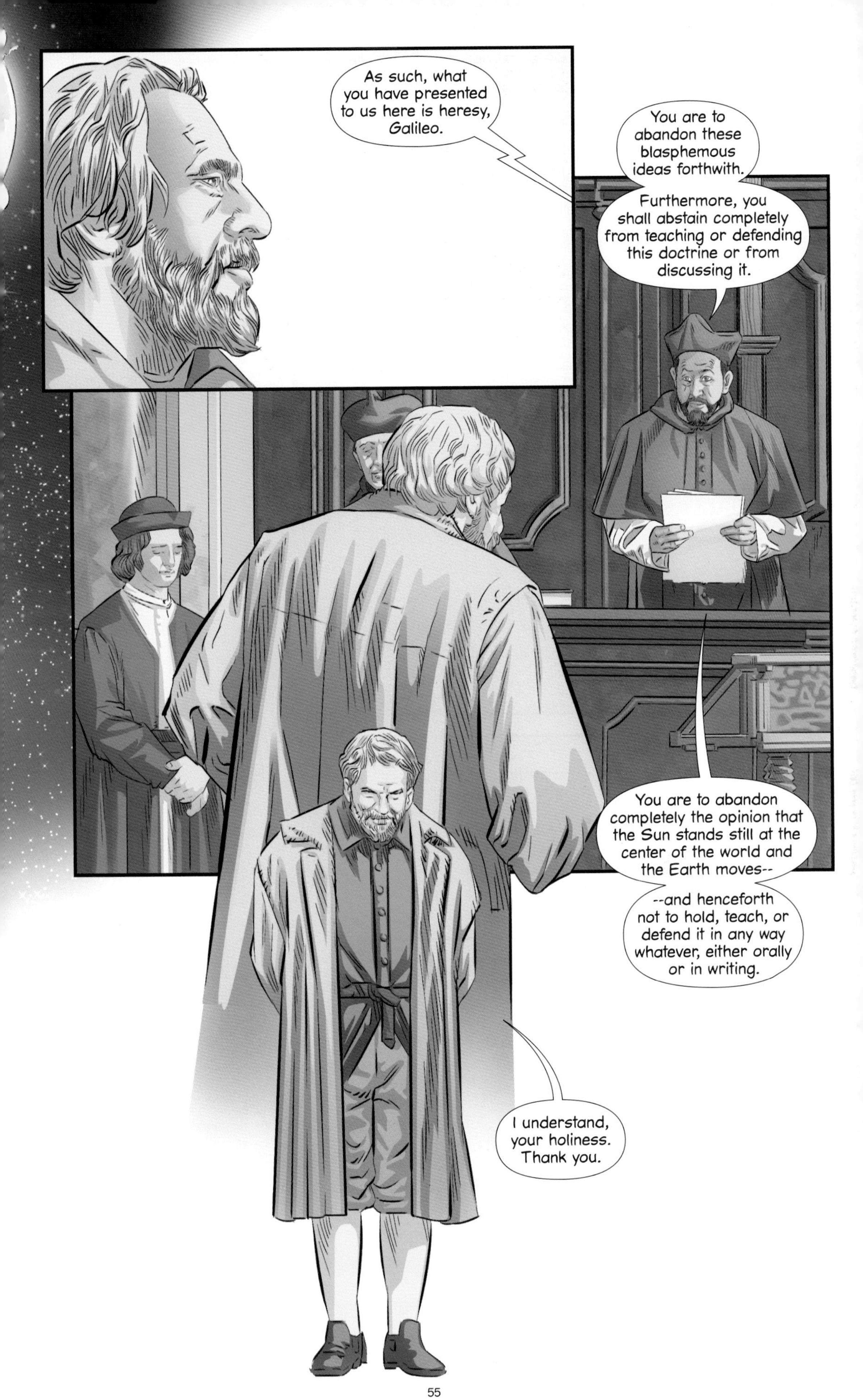

As such, what you have presented to us here is heresy, Galileo.
You are to abandon these blasphemous ideas forthwith.
Furthermore, you shall abstain completely from teaching or defending this doctrine or from discussing it.
You are to abandon completely the opinion that the Sun stands still at the center of the world and the Earth moves--
--and henceforth not to hold, teach, or defend it in any way whatever, either orally or in writing.
I understand, your holiness. Thank you.

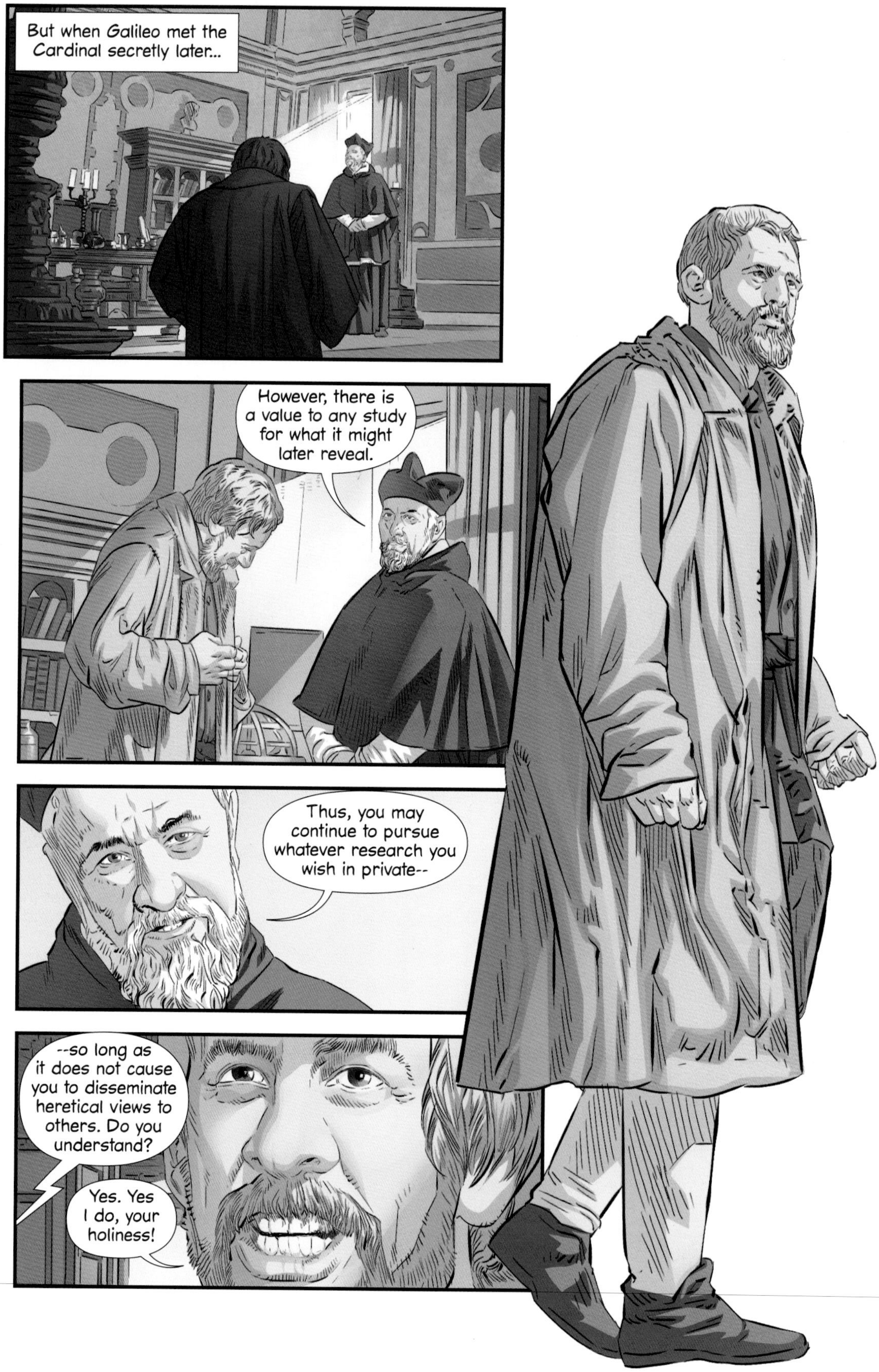
But when Galileo met the Cardinal secretly later...
However, there is a value to any study for what it might later reveal.
Thus, you may continue to pursue whatever research you wish in private--
--so long as it does not cause you to disseminate heretical views to others. Do you understand?
Yes. Yes I do, your holiness!

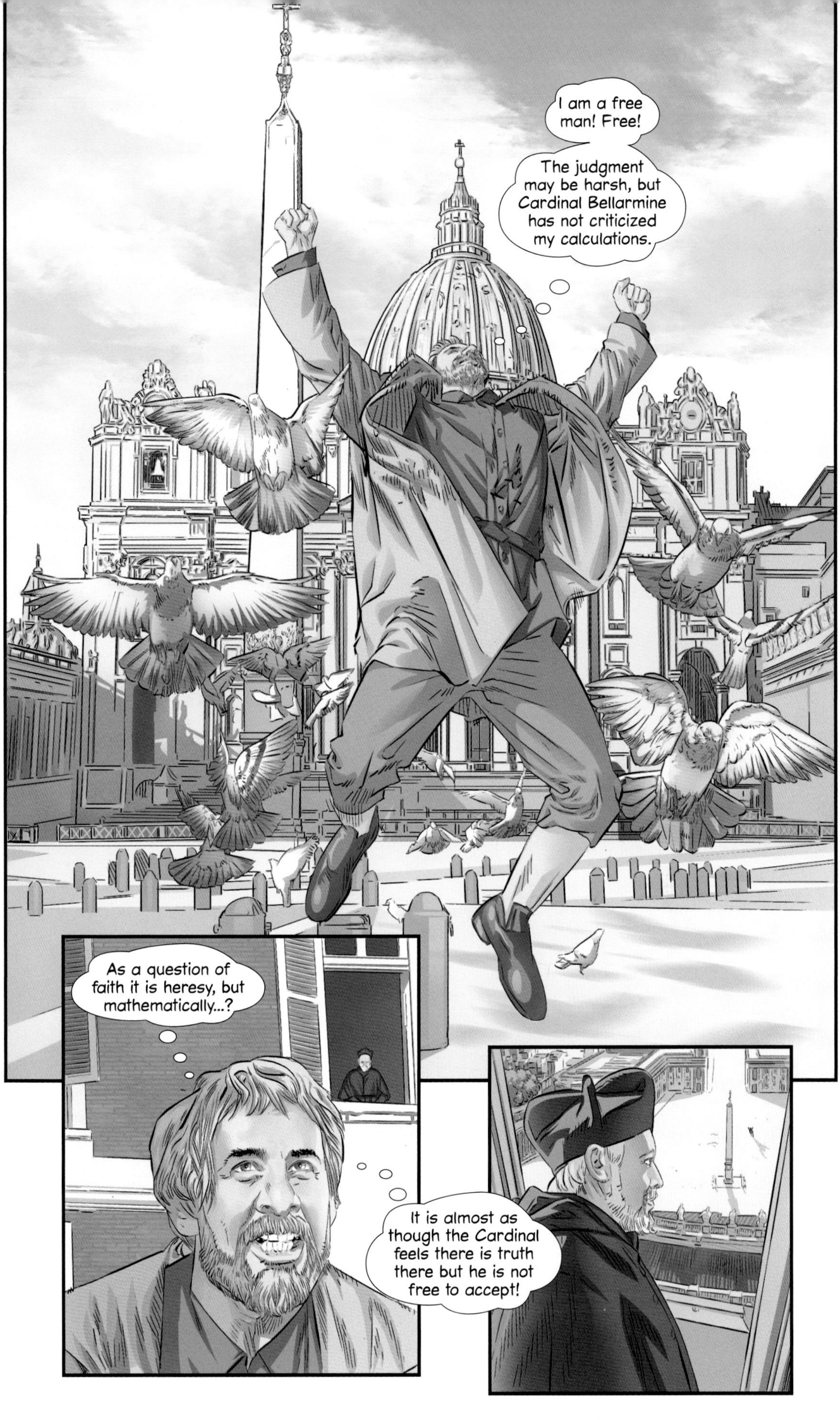
I am a free man! Free!
The judgment may be harsh, but Cardinal Bellarmine has not criticized my calculations.
As a question of faith it is heresy, but mathematically...?
It is almost as though the Cardinal feels there is truth there but he is not free to accept!

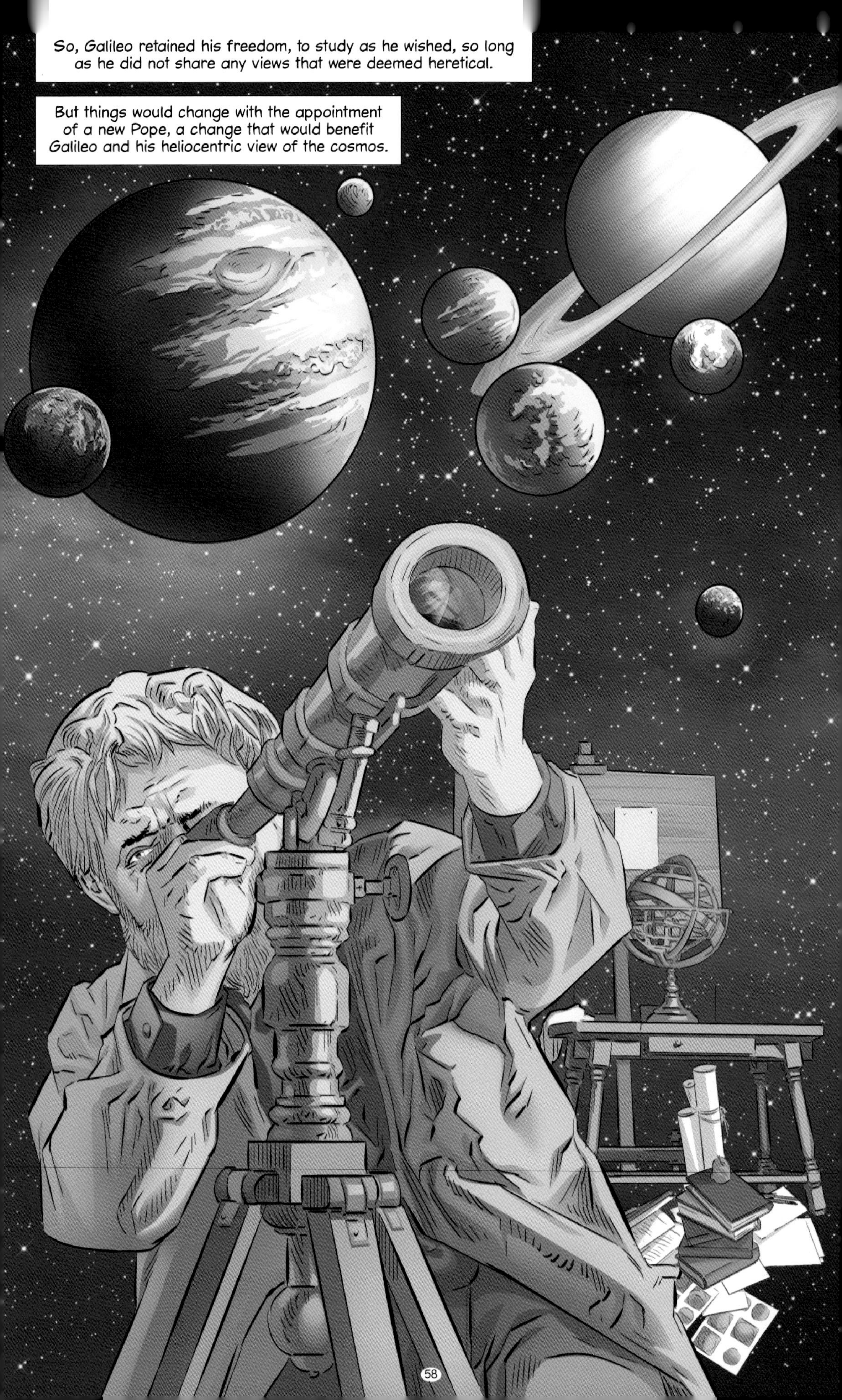
So, Galileo retained his freedom, to study as he wished, so long as he did not share any views that were deemed heretical.
But things would change with the appointment of a new Pope, a change that would benefit Galileo and his heliocentric view of the cosmos.

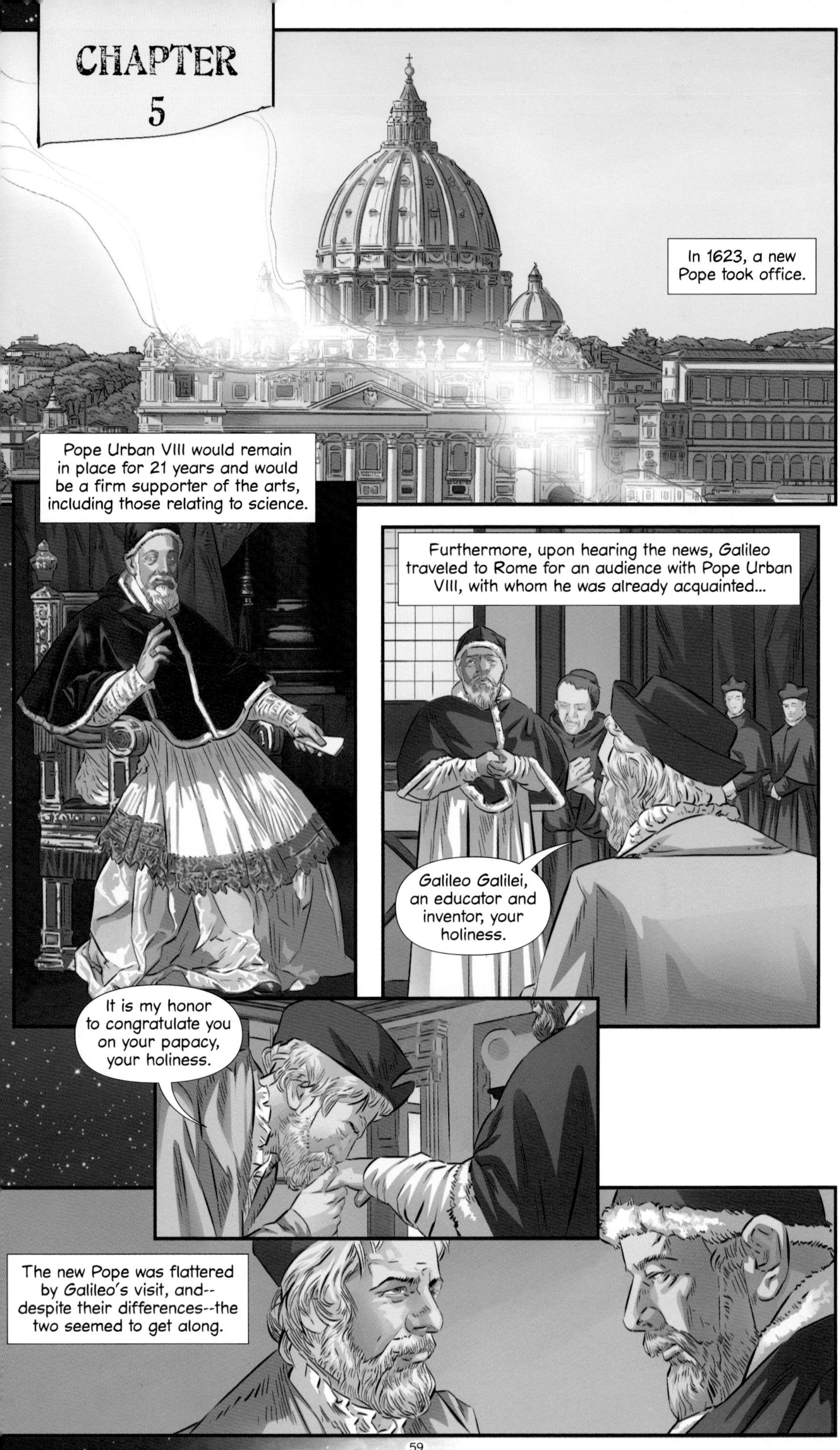
CHAPTER 5
In 1623, a new Pope took office.
Pope Urban VIII would remain in place for 21 years and would be a firm supporter of the arts, including those relating to science.
Furthermore, upon hearing the news, Galileo traveled to Rome for an audience with Pope Urban VIII, with whom he was already acquainted...
Galileo Galilei, an educator and inventor, your holiness.
It is my honor to congratulate you on your papacy, your holiness.
The new Pope was flattered by Galileo's visit, and--despite their differences--the two seemed to get along.

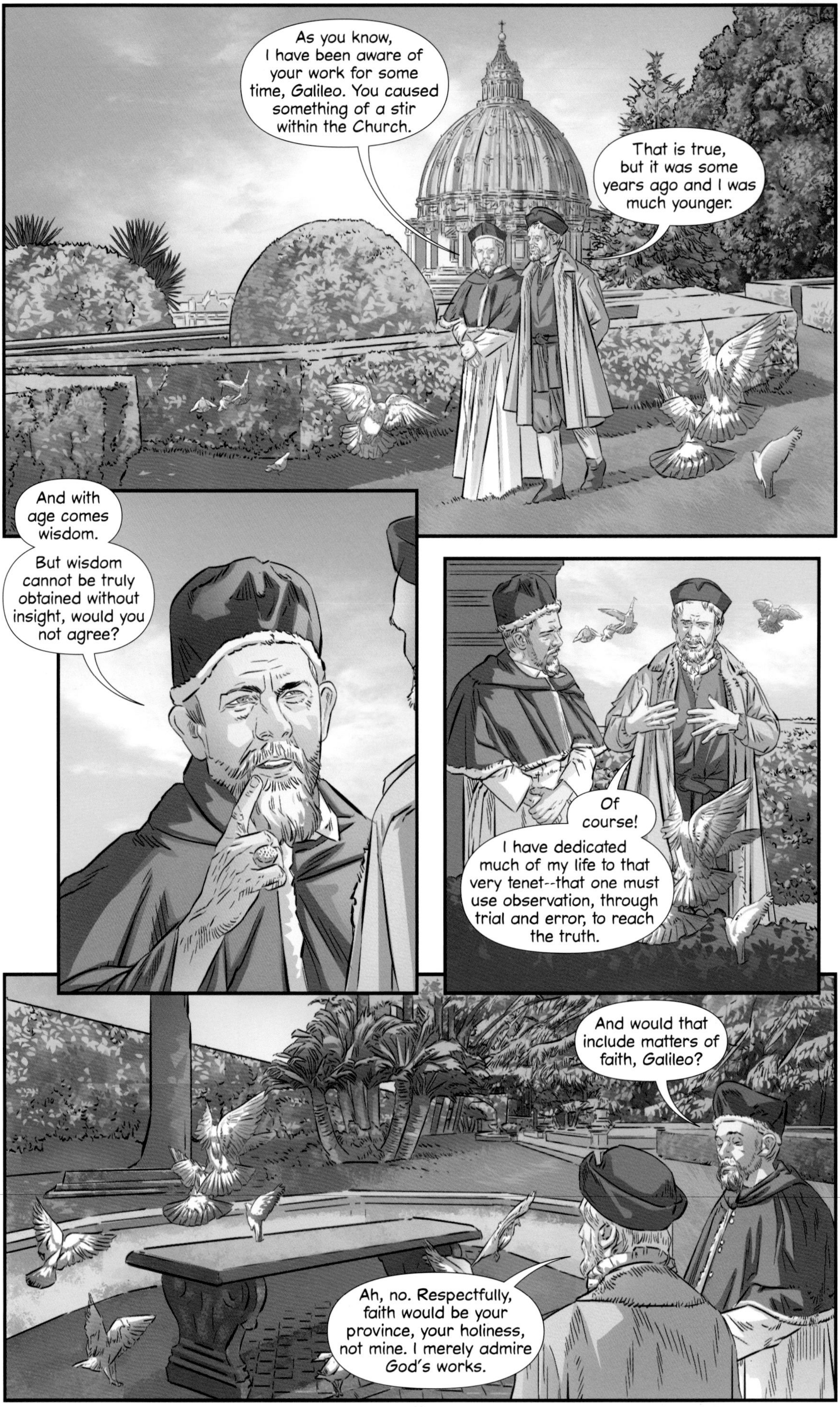

As you know, I have been aware of your work for some time, Galileo. You caused something of a stir within the Church.
That is true, but it was some years ago and I was much younger.
And with age comes wisdom.
But wisdom cannot be truly obtained without insight, would you not agree?
Of course!
I have dedicated much of my life to that very tenet--that one must use observation, through trial and error, to reach the truth.
And would that include matters of faith, Galileo?
Ah, no. Respectfully, faith would be your province, your holiness, not mine. I merely admire God's works.

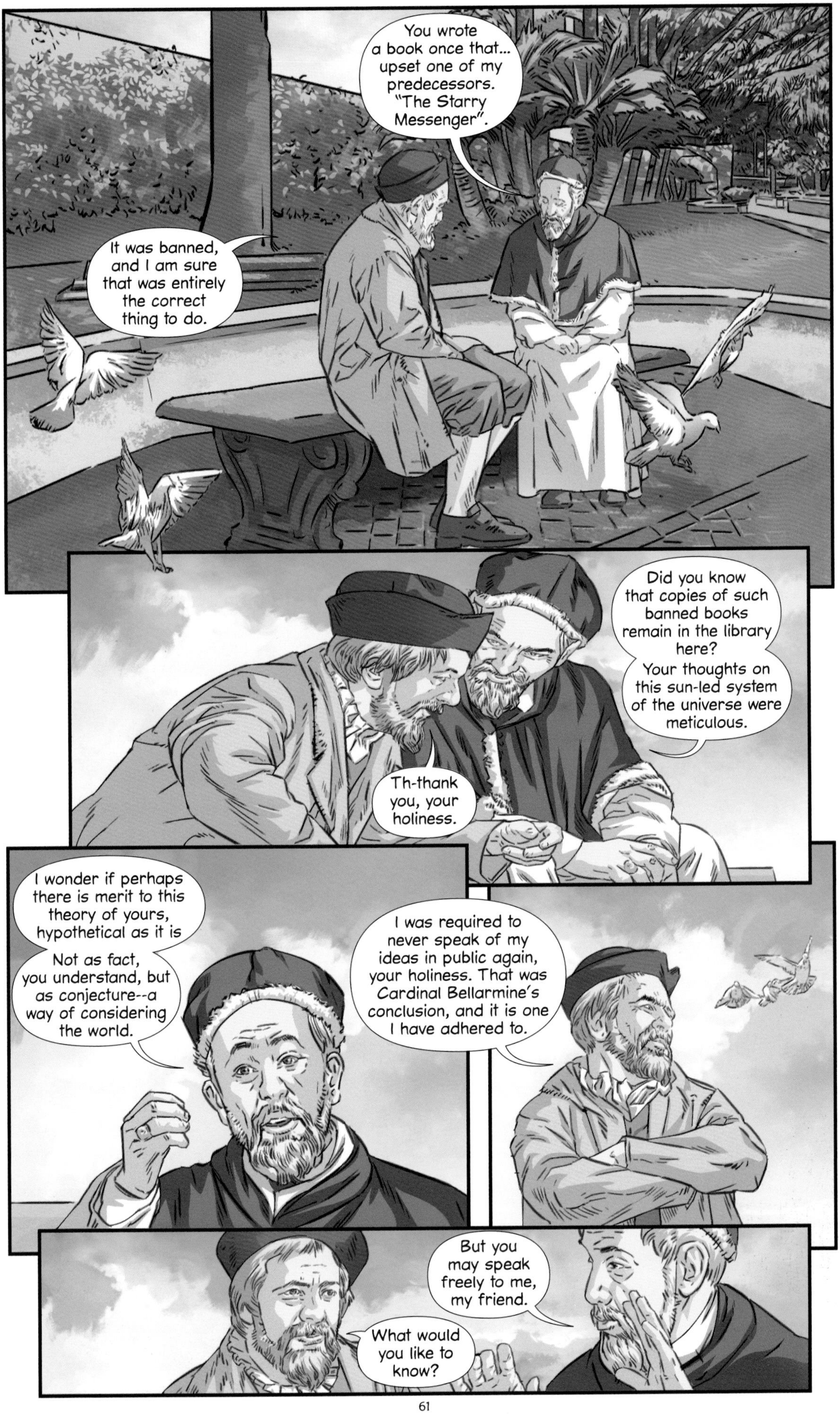
You wrote a book once that... upset one of my predecessors. "The Starry Messenger".
It was banned, and I am sure that was entirely the correct thing to do.
Did you know that copies of such banned books remain in the library here?
Your thoughts on this sun-led system of the universe were meticulous.
Th-thank you, your holiness.
I wonder if perhaps there is merit to this theory of yours, hypothetical as it is
Not as fact, you understand, but as conjecture--a way of considering the world.
I was required to never speak of my ideas in public again, your holiness. That was Cardinal Bellarmine's conclusion, and it is one I have adhered to.
But you may speak freely to me, my friend.
What would you like to know?

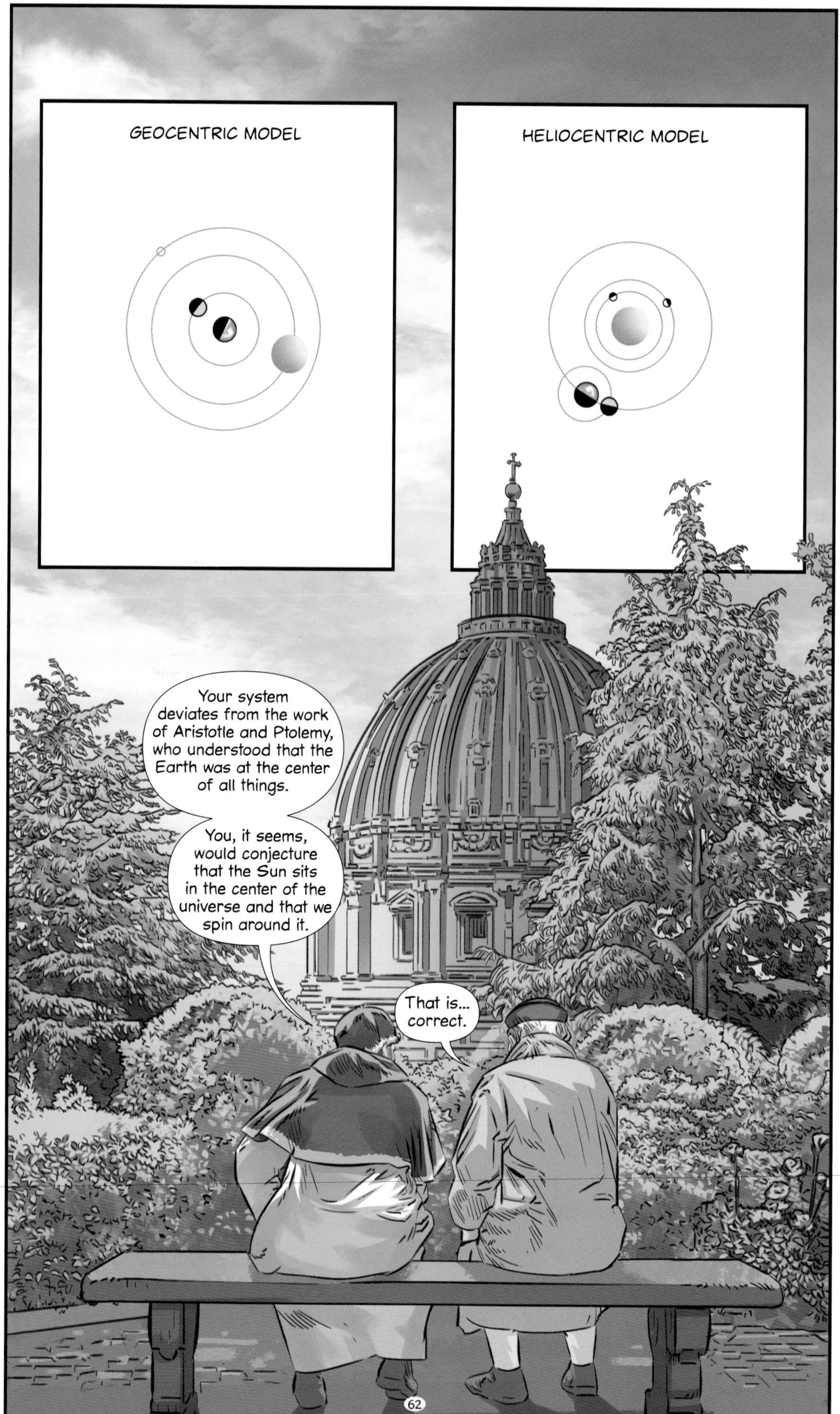
GEOCENTRIC MODEL
HELIOCENTRIC MODEL
Your system deviates from the work of Aristotle and Ptolemy, who understood that the Earth was at the center of all things.
You, it seems, would conjecture that the Sun sits in the center of the universe and that we spin around it.
That is... correct.

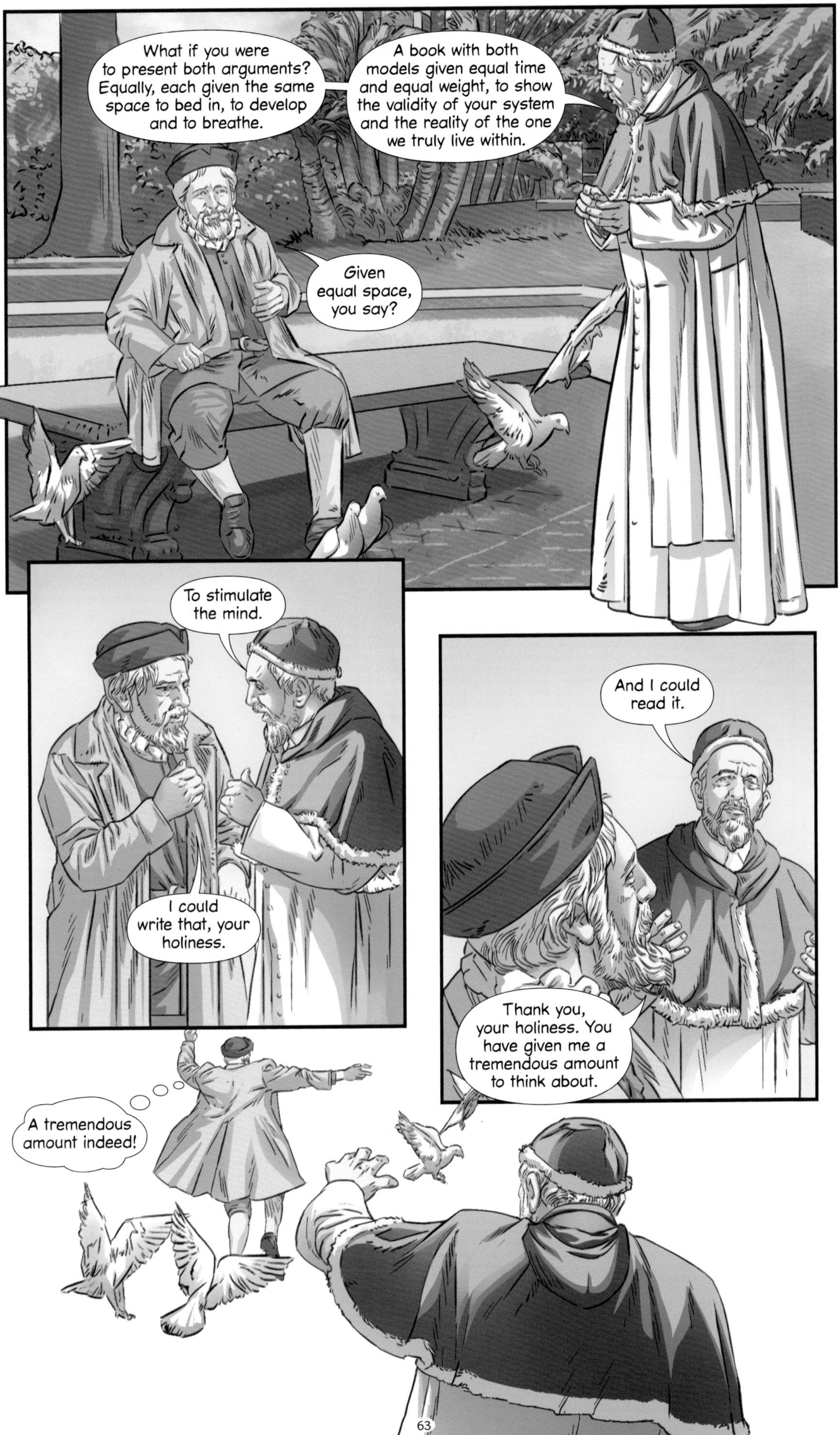
What if you were to present both arguments? Equally, each given the same space to bed in, to develop and to breathe.
A book with both models given equal time and equal weight, to show the validity of your system and the reality of the one we truly live within.
Given equal space, you say?
To stimulate the mind.
I could write that, your holiness.
And I could read it.
Thank you, your holiness. You have given me a tremendous amount to think about.
A tremendous amount indeed!

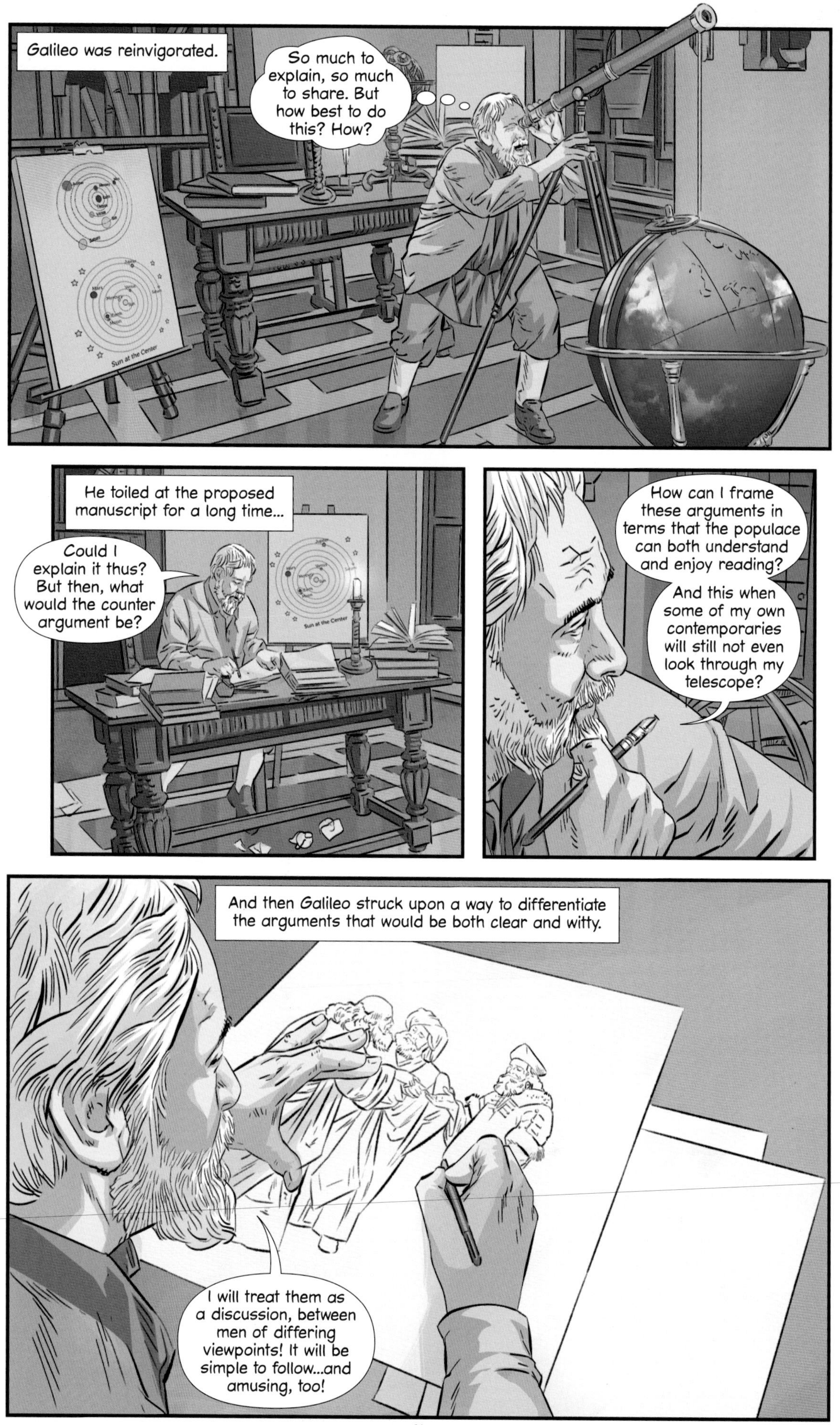
Galileo was reinvigorated.
So much to explain, so much to share. But how best to do this? How?
Sun at the Center
He toiled at the proposed manuscript for a long time...
Could I explain it thus? But then, what would the counter argument be?
Sun at the Center
How can I frame these arguments in terms that the populace can both understand and enjoy reading?
And this when some of my own contemporaries will still not even look through my telescope?
And then Galileo struck upon a way to differentiate the arguments that would be both clear and witty.
I will treat them as a discussion, between men of differing viewpoints! It will be simple to follow...and amusing, too!

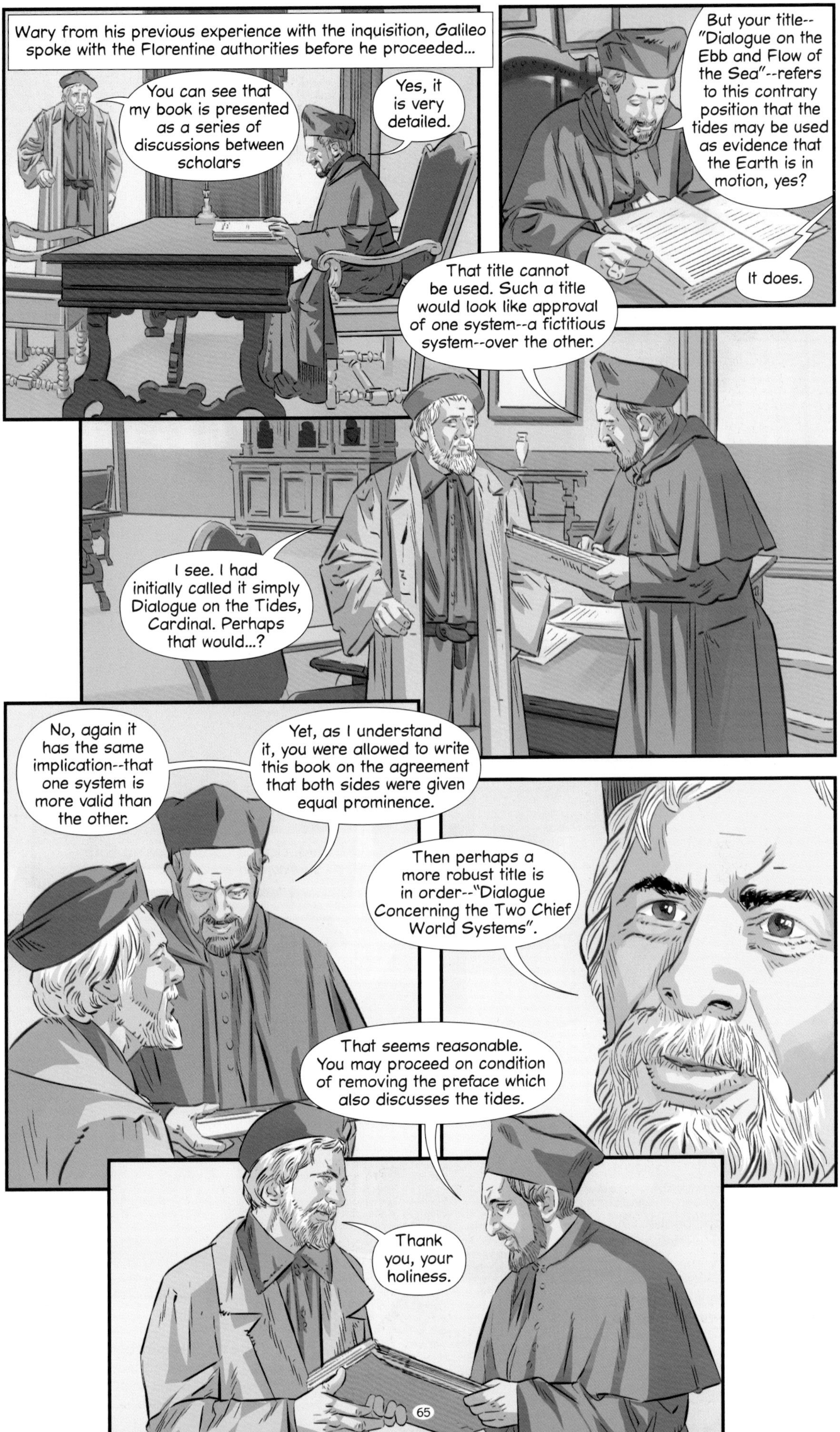
Wary from his previous experience with the inquisition, Galileo spoke with the Florentine authorities before he proceeded...
You can see that my book is presented as a series of discussions between scholars
Yes, it is very detailed.
But your title--"Dialogue on the Ebb and Flow of the Sea"--refers to this contrary position that the tides may be used as evidence that the Earth is in motion, yes?
It does.
That title cannot be used. Such a title would look like approval of one system--a fictitious system--over the other.
I see. I had initially called it simply Dialogue on the Tides, Cardinal. Perhaps that would...?
No, again it has the same implication--that one system is more valid than the other.
Yet, as I understand it, you were allowed to write this book on the agreement that both sides were given equal prominence.
Then perhaps a more robust title is in order--"Dialogue Concerning the Two Chief World Systems".
That seems reasonable. You may proceed on condition of removing the preface which also discusses the tides.
Thank you, your holiness.

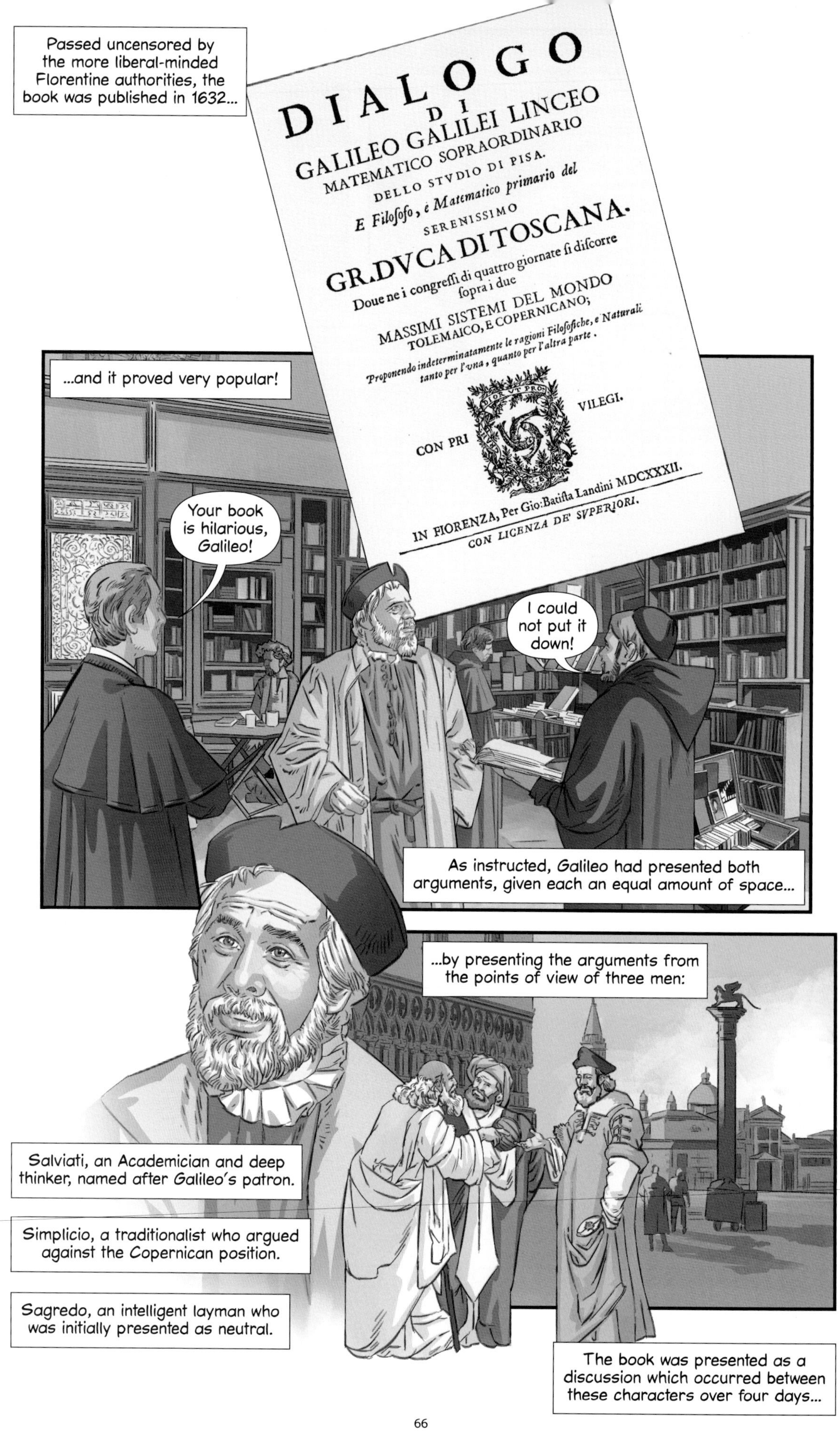
Passed uncensored by the more liberal-minded Florentine authorities, the book was published in 1632...
DIALOGO
DI
GALILEO GALILEI LINCEO
MATEMATICO SOPRAORDINARIO
DELLO STVDIO DI PISA.
E Filosofo, e Matematico primario del
SERENISSIMO
GR.DVCA DI TOSCANA.
Doue ne i congressi di quattro giornate si discorre
sopra i due
MASSIMI SISTEMI DEL MONDO
TOLEMAICO, E COPERNICANO;
Proponendo indeterminatamente le ragioni Filosofiche, e Naturali
tanto per l'vna, quanto per l'altra parte.
CON PRIVILEGI.
IN FIORENZA, Per Gio: Batista Landini MDCXXXII.
CON LICENZA DE' SVPERIORI.
...and it proved very popular!
Your book is hilarious, Galileo!
I could not put it down!
As instructed, Galileo had presented both arguments, given each an equal amount of space...
...by presenting the arguments from the points of view of three men:
Salviati, an Academician and deep thinker, named after Galileo's patron.
Simplicio, a traditionalist who argued against the Copernican position.
Sagredo, an intelligent layman who was initially presented as neutral.
The book was presented as a discussion which occurred between these characters over four days...

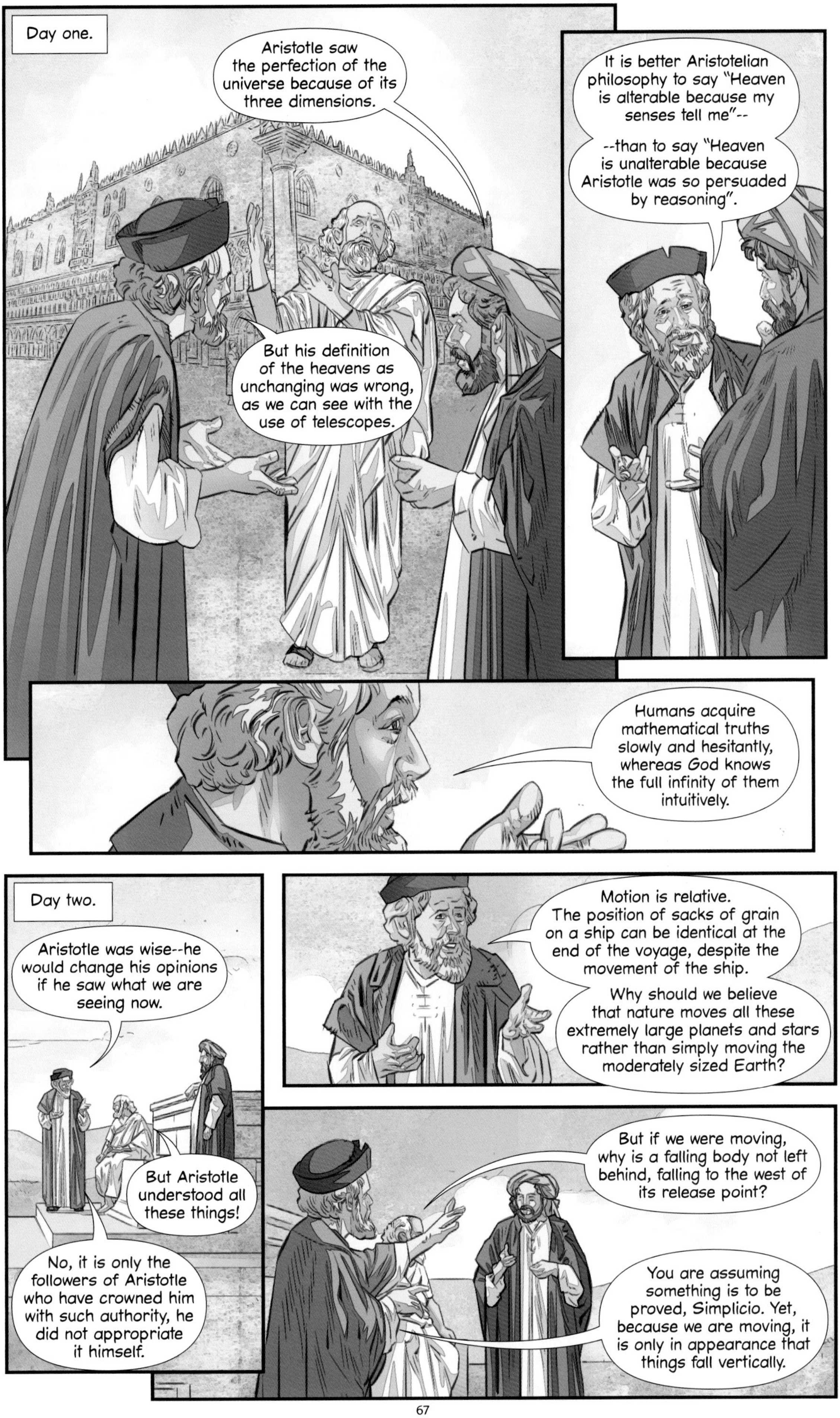
Day one.
Aristotle saw the perfection of the universe because of its three dimensions.
But his definition of the heavens as unchanging was wrong, as we can see with the use of telescopes.
It is better Aristotelian philosophy to say "Heaven is alterable because my senses tell me"--
--than to say "Heaven is unalterable because Aristotle was so persuaded by reasoning".
Humans acquire mathematical truths slowly and hesitantly, whereas God knows the full infinity of them intuitively.
Day two.
Aristotle was wise--he would change his opinions if he saw what we are seeing now.
But Aristotle understood all these things!
No, it is only the followers of Aristotle who have crowned him with such authority, he did not appropriate it himself.
Motion is relative. The position of sacks of grain on a ship can be identical at the end of the voyage, despite the movement of the ship.
Why should we believe that nature moves all these extremely large planets and stars rather than simply moving the moderately sized Earth?
But if we were moving, why is a falling body not left behind, falling to the west of its release point?
You are assuming something is to be proved, Simplicio. Yet, because we are moving, it is only in appearance that things fall vertically.

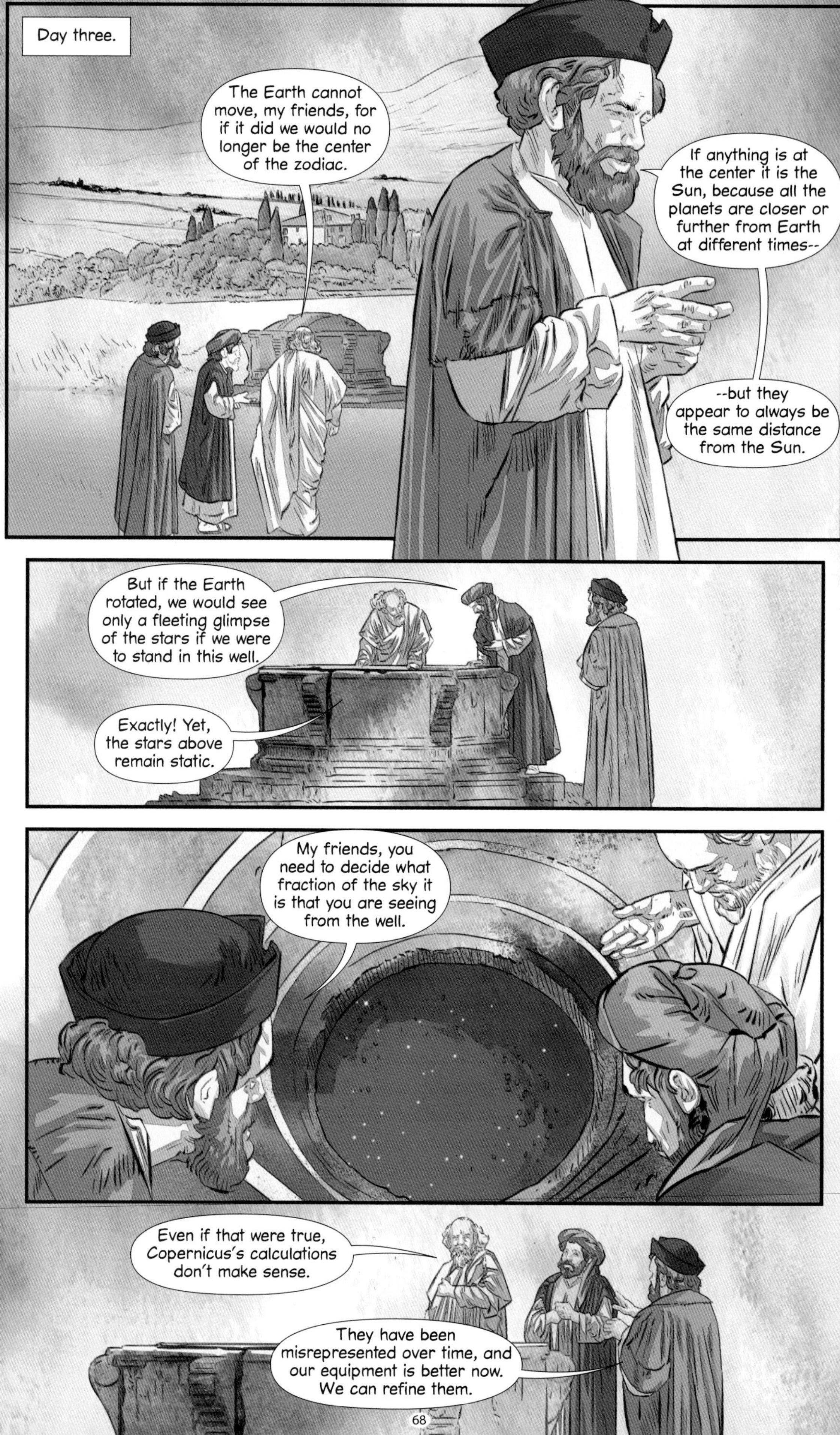
Day three.
The Earth cannot move, my friends, for if it did we would no longer be the center of the zodiac.
If anything is at the center it is the Sun, because all the planets are closer or further from Earth at different times--
--but they appear to always be the same distance from the Sun.
But if the Earth rotated, we would see only a fleeting glimpse of the stars if we were to stand in this well.
Exactly! Yet, the stars above remain static.
My friends, you need to decide what fraction of the sky it is that you are seeing from the well.
Even if that were true, Copernicus's calculations don't make sense.
They have been misrepresented over time, and our equipment is better now. We can refine them.

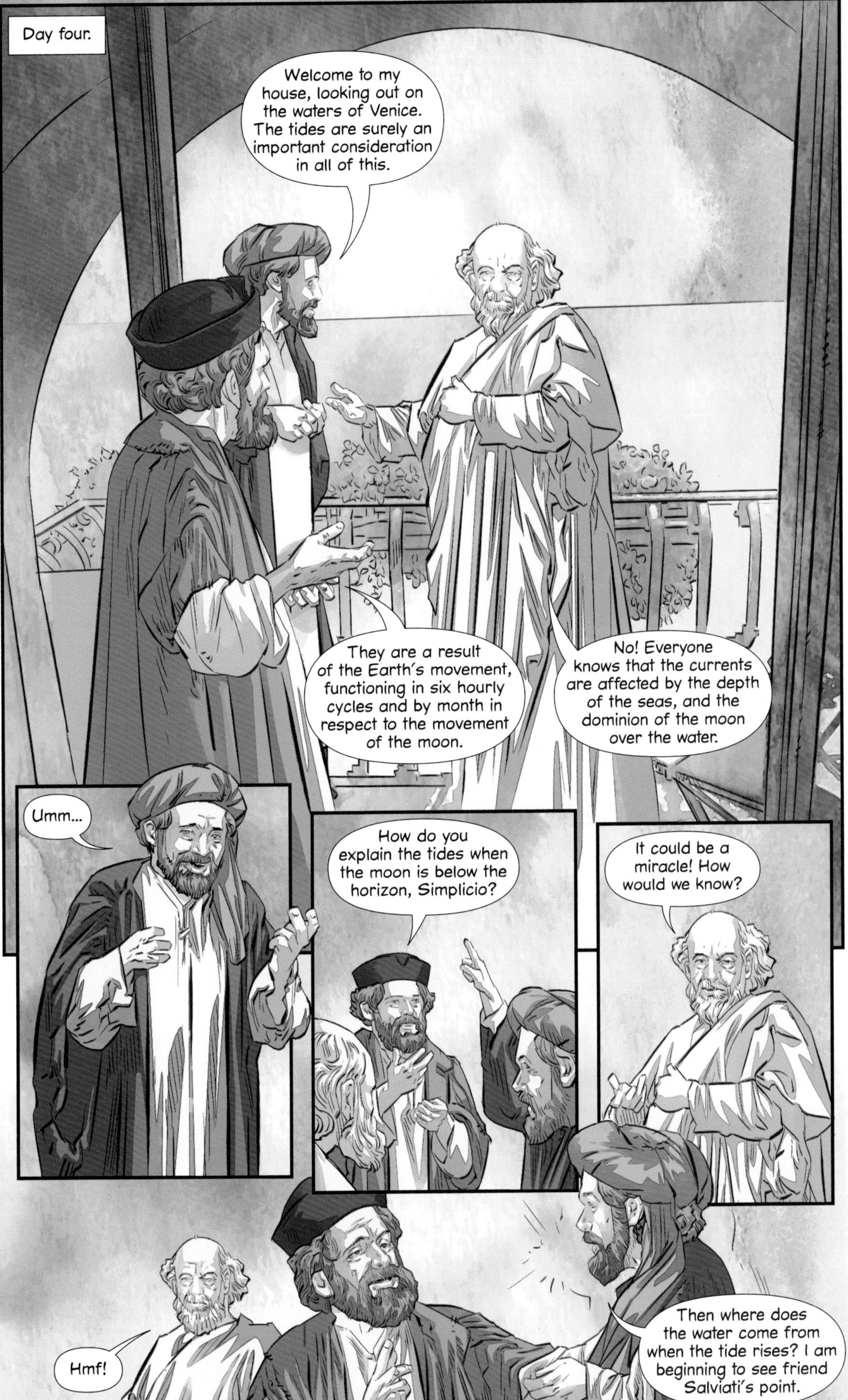
Day four.
Welcome to my house, looking out on the waters of Venice. The tides are surely an important consideration in all of this.
They are a result of the Earth's movement, functioning in six hourly cycles and by month in respect to the movement of the moon.
No! Everyone knows that the currents are affected by the depth of the seas, and the dominion of the moon over the water.
Umm...
How do you explain the tides when the moon is below the horizon, Simplicio?
It could be a miracle! How would we know?
Hmf!
Then where does the water come from when the tide rises? I am beginning to see friend Salviati's point.

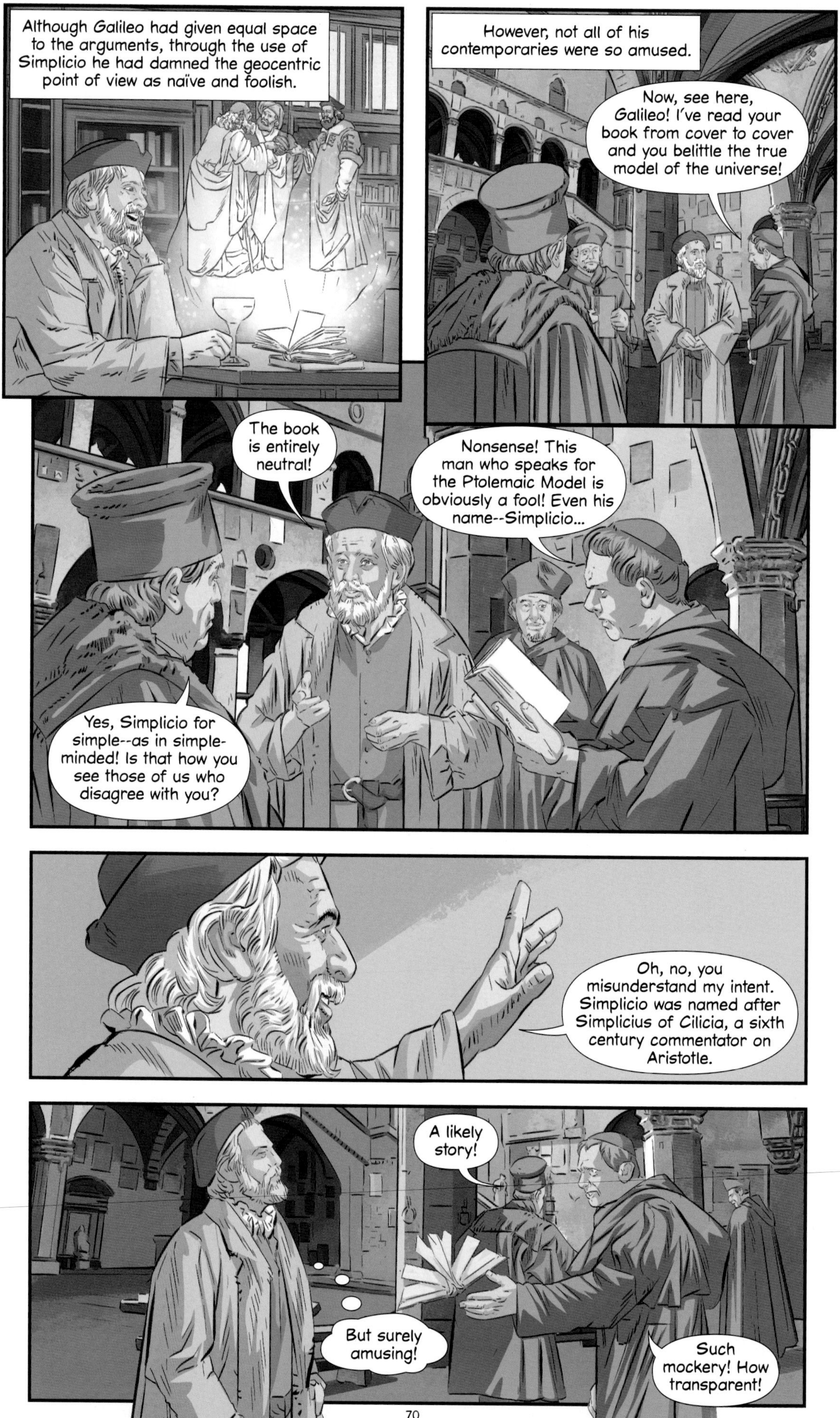
Although Galileo had given equal space to the arguments, through the use of Simplicio he had damned the geocentric point of view as naïve and foolish.
However, not all of his contemporaries were so amused.
Now, see here, Galileo! I've read your book from cover to cover and you belittle the true model of the universe!
The book is entirely neutral!
Nonsense! This man who speaks for the Ptolemaic Model is obviously a fool! Even his name--Simplicio...
Yes, Simplicio for simple--as in simple-minded! Is that how you see those of us who disagree with you?
Oh, no, you misunderstand my intent. Simplicio was named after Simplicius of Cilicia, a sixth century commentator on Aristotle.
A likely story!
But surely amusing!
Such mockery! How transparent!

However, Pope Urban VIII was not amused.

I asked Galileo to fairly include the geocentric view--my view and the view of the church--in his book so that he might make his argument.

But he has placed that view into the mouth of this Simplicio! A fool by any other name!

This is a snub to everything we agreed to.

Shortly after, sale of the book was banned by the Catholic Church

My books!

We shall be taking these, sir. Every copy you have!

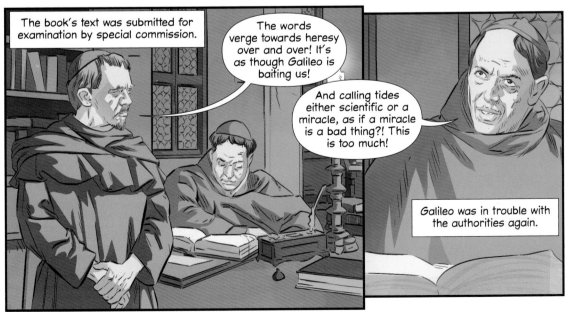

The book's text was submitted for examination by special commission.

The words verge towards heresy over and over! It's as though Galileo is baiting us!

And calling tides either scientific or a miracle, as if a miracle is a bad thing?! This is too much!

Galileo was in trouble with the authorities again.

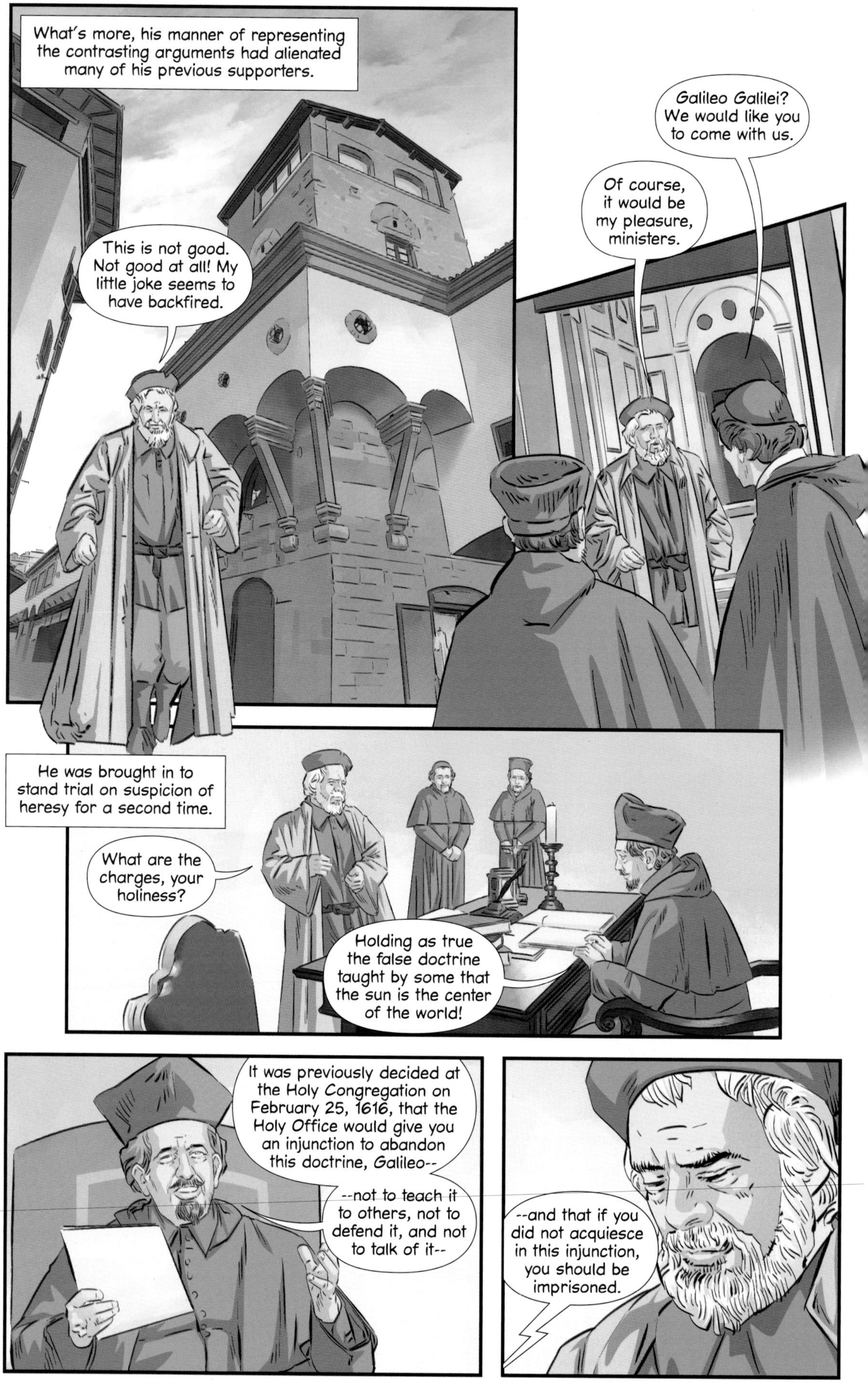
What's more, his manner of representing the contrasting arguments had alienated many of his previous supporters.
This is not good. Not good at all! My little joke seems to have backfired.
Galileo Galilei? We would like you to come with us.
Of course, it would be my pleasure, ministers.
He was brought in to stand trial on suspicion of heresy for a second time.
What are the charges, your holiness?
Holding as true the false doctrine taught by some that the sun is the center of the world!
It was previously decided at the Holy Congregation on February 25, 1616, that the Holy Office would give you an injunction to abandon this doctrine, Galileo--
--not to teach it to others, not to defend it, and not to talk of it--
--and that if you did not acquiesce in this injunction, you should be imprisoned.

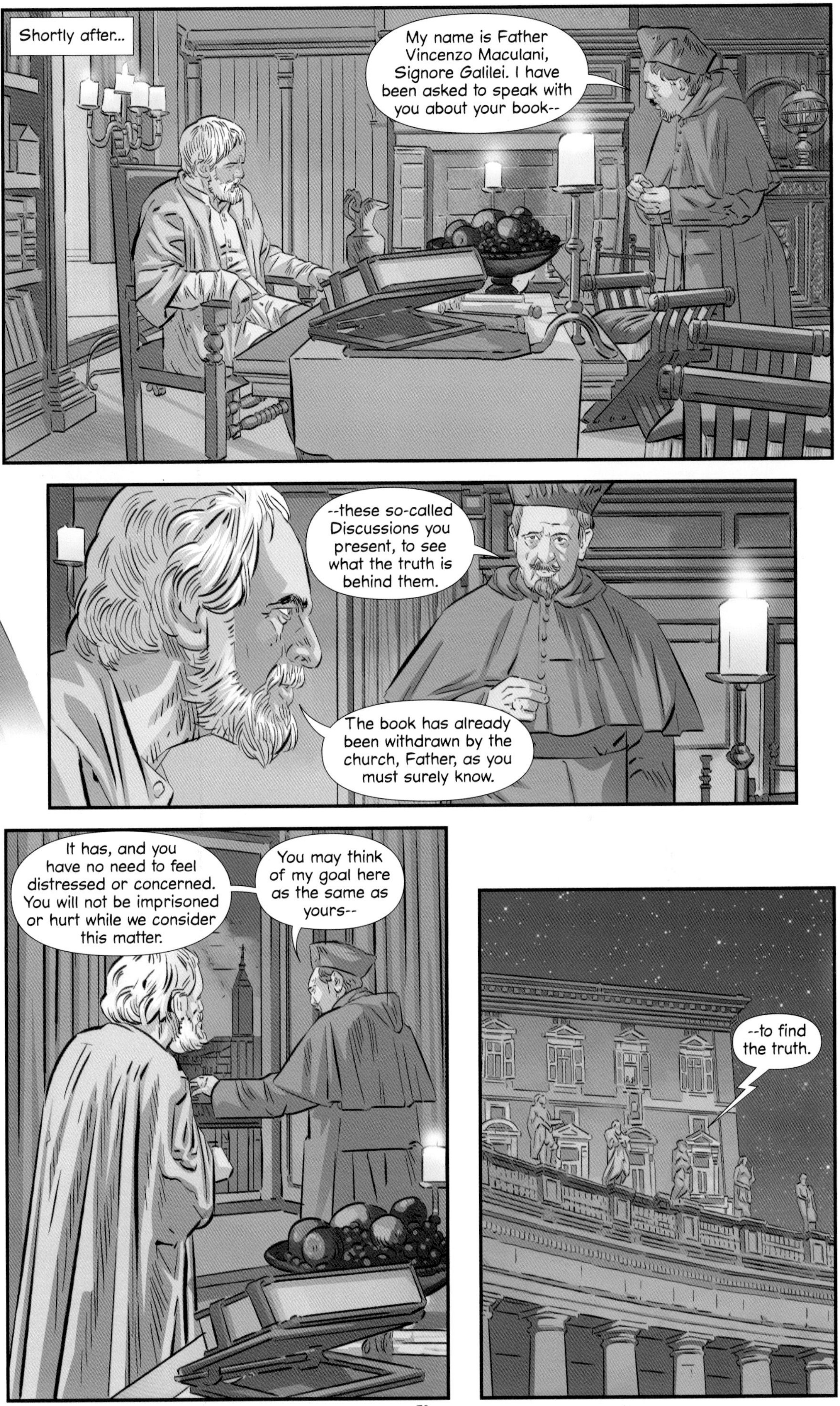
Shortly after...
My name is Father Vincenzo Maculani, Signore Galilei. I have been asked to speak with you about your book--
--these so-called Discussions you present, to see what the truth is behind them.
The book has already been withdrawn by the church, Father, as you must surely know.
It has, and you have no need to feel distressed or concerned. You will not be imprisoned or hurt while we consider this matter.
You may think of my goal here as the same as yours--
--to find the truth.

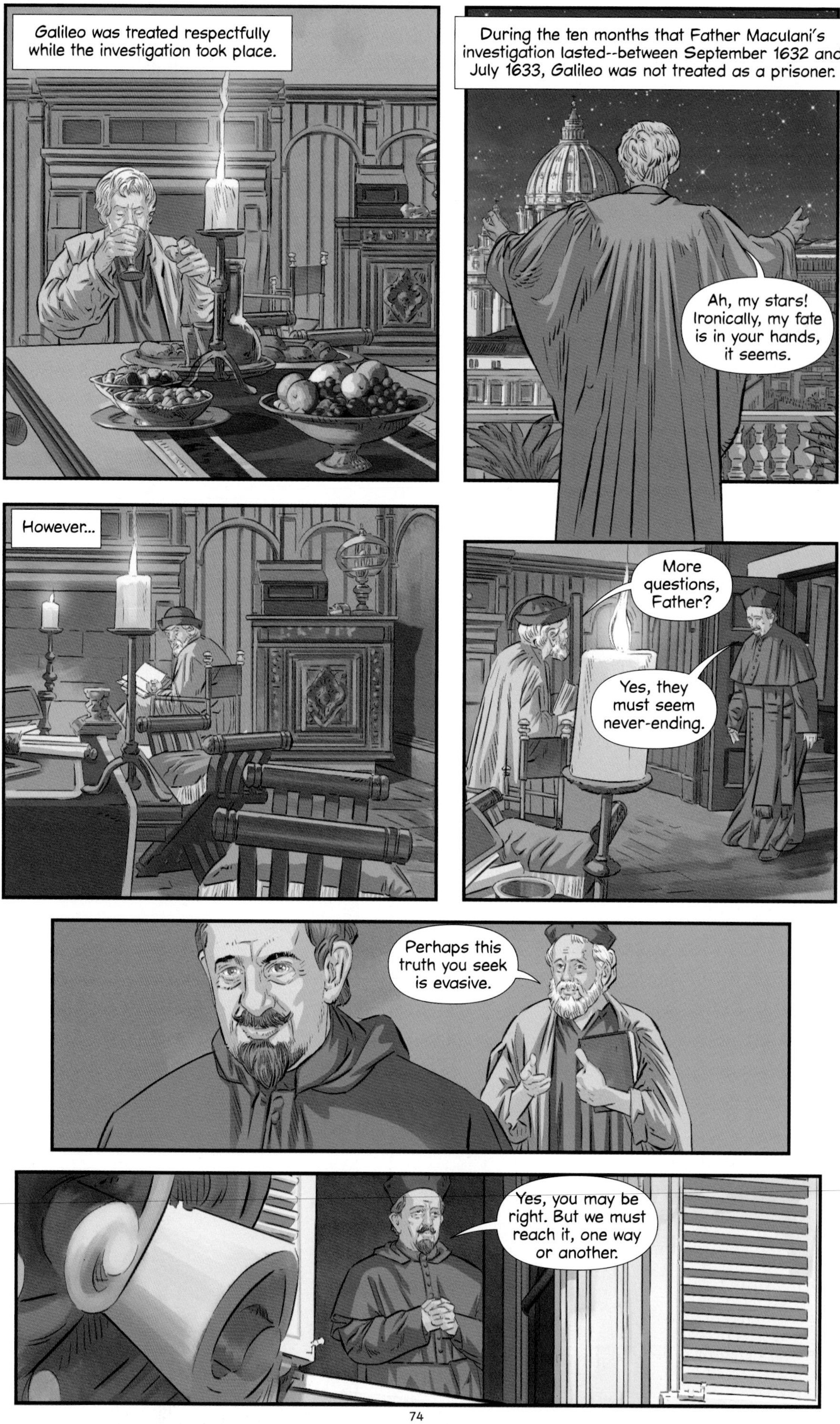
Galileo was treated respectfully while the investigation took place.
During the ten months that Father Maculani's investigation lasted--between September 1632 and July 1633, Galileo was not treated as a prisoner.
Ah, my stars! Ironically, my fate is in your hands, it seems.
However...
More questions, Father?
Yes, they must seem never-ending.
Perhaps this truth you seek is evasive.
Yes, you may be right. But we must reach it, one way or another.

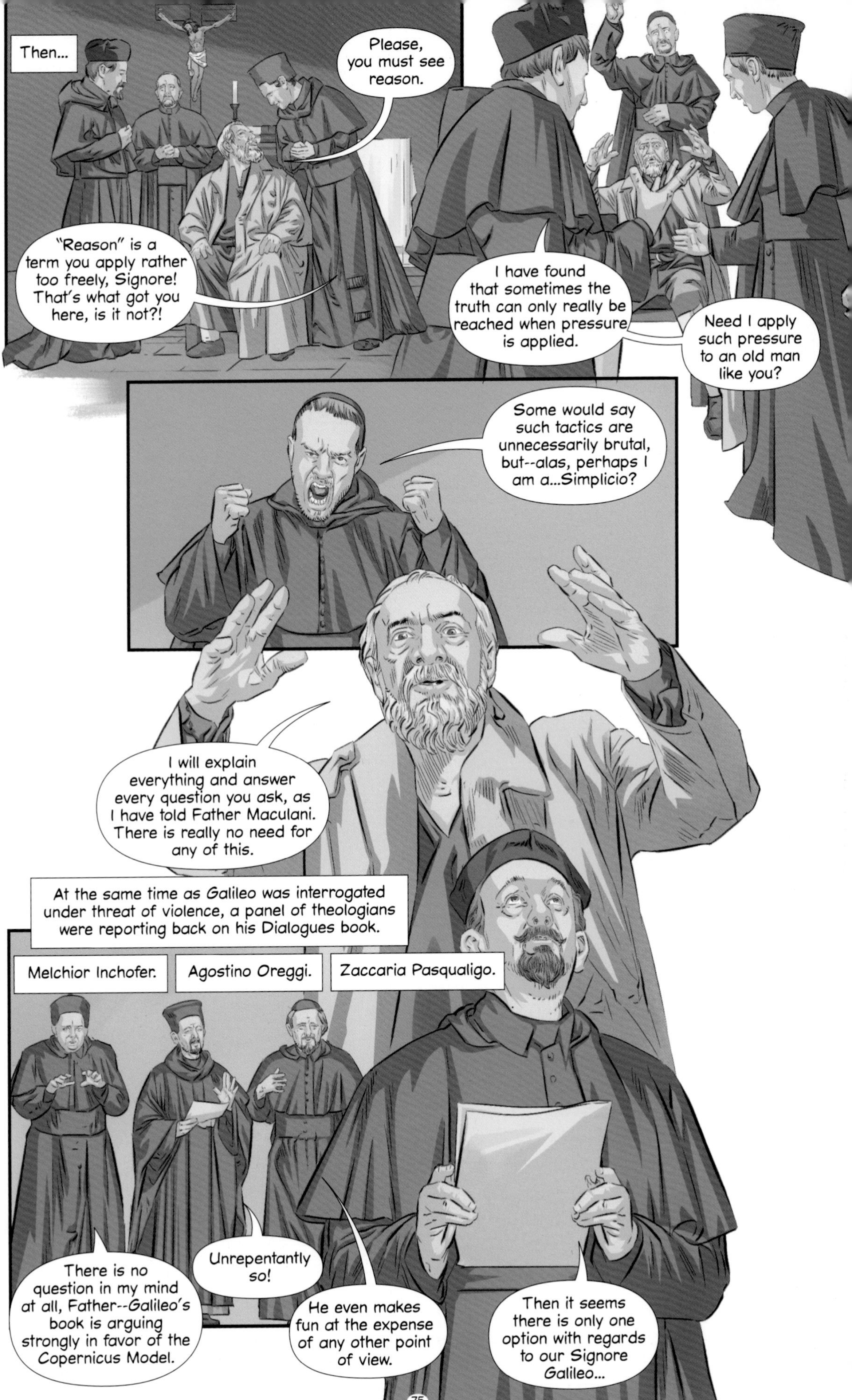
Then...
Please, you must see reason.
"Reason" is a term you apply rather too freely, Signore! That's what got you here, is it not?!
I have found that sometimes the truth can only really be reached when pressure is applied.
Need I apply such pressure to an old man like you?
Some would say such tactics are unnecessarily brutal, but--alas, perhaps I am a...Simplicio?
I will explain everything and answer every question you ask, as I have told Father Maculani. There is really no need for any of this.
At the same time as Galileo was interrogated under threat of violence, a panel of theologians were reporting back on his Dialogues book.
Melchior Inchofer.
Agostino Oreggi.
Zaccaria Pasqualigo.
There is no question in my mind at all, Father--Galileo's book is arguing strongly in favor of the Copernicus Model.
Unrepentantly so!
He even makes fun at the expense of any other point of view.
Then it seems there is only one option with regards to our Signore Galileo...

Sentence was passed on June 22, 1633...
Galileo Galilei, you are found vehemently suspect of heresy--
--specifically holding the opinion that the Sun lies motionless at the center of the universe, that the Earth is not at its center and moves--
--and that one may hold and defend an opinion as probable after it has been declared contrary to Holy Scripture.

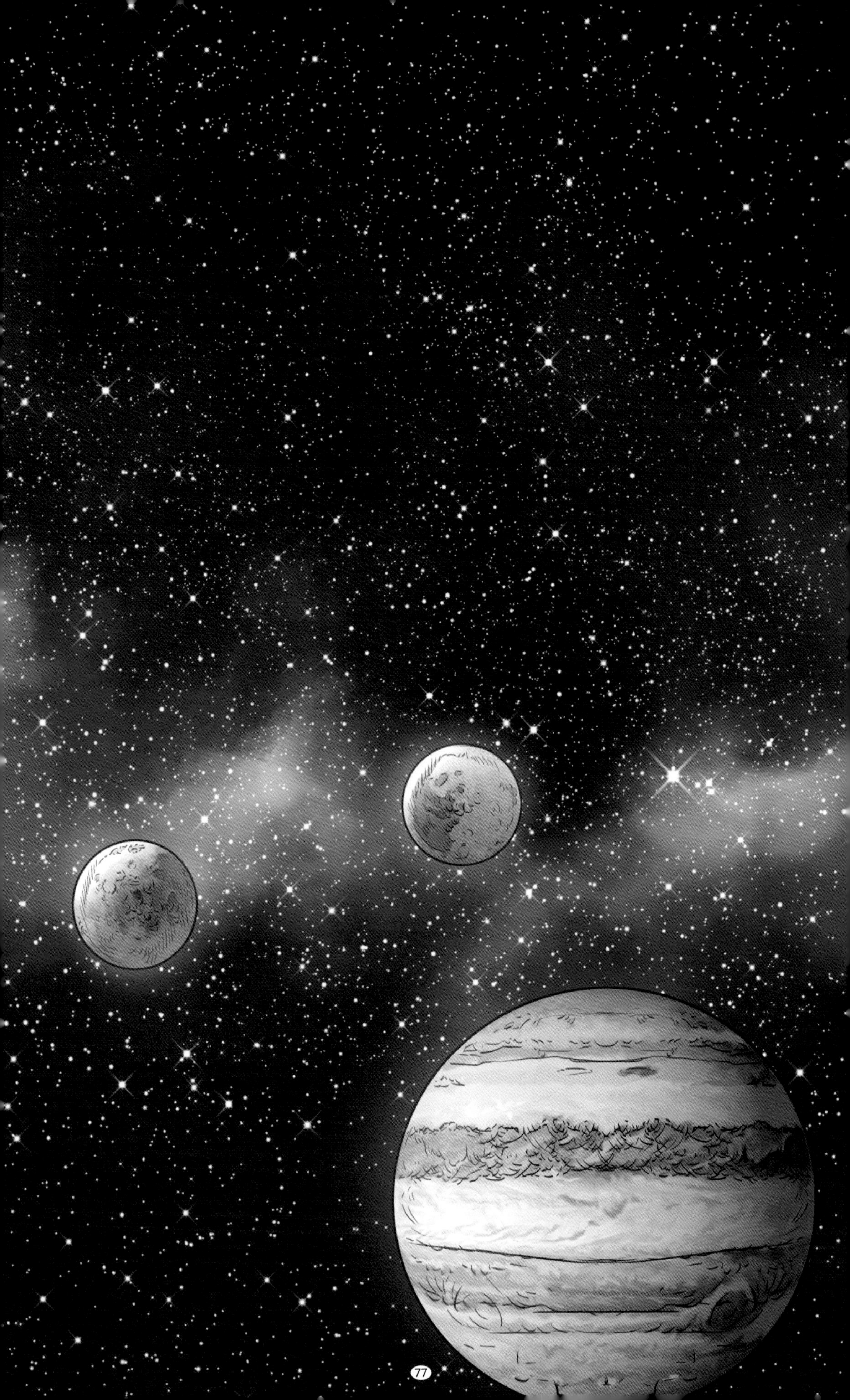

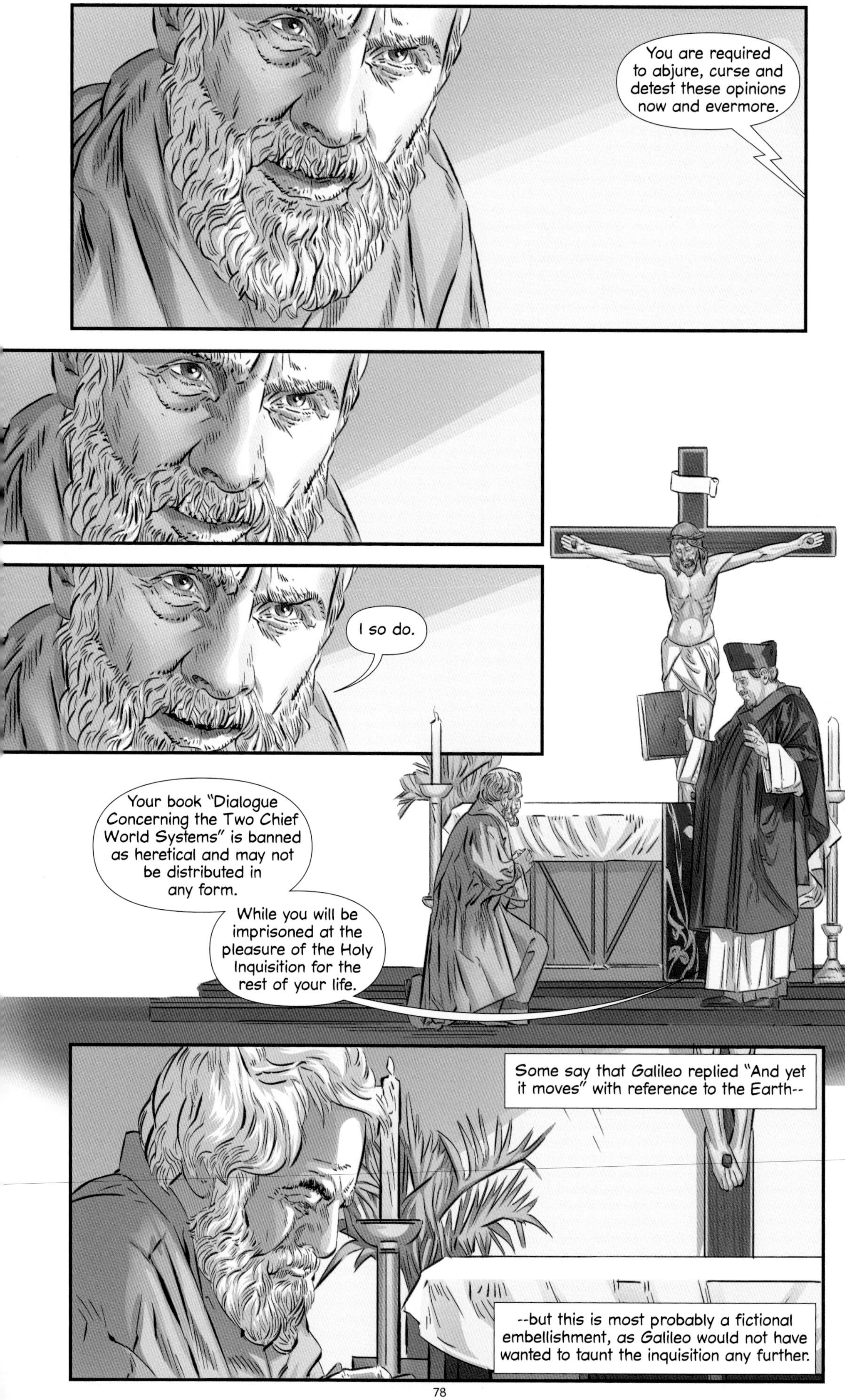
You are required to abjure, curse and detest these opinions now and evermore.
I so do.
Your book "Dialogue Concerning the Two Chief World Systems" is banned as heretical and may not be distributed in any form.
While you will be imprisoned at the pleasure of the Holy Inquisition for the rest of your life.
Some say that Galileo replied "And yet it moves" with reference to the Earth--
--but this is most probably a fictional embellishment, as Galileo would not have wanted to taunt the inquisition any further.

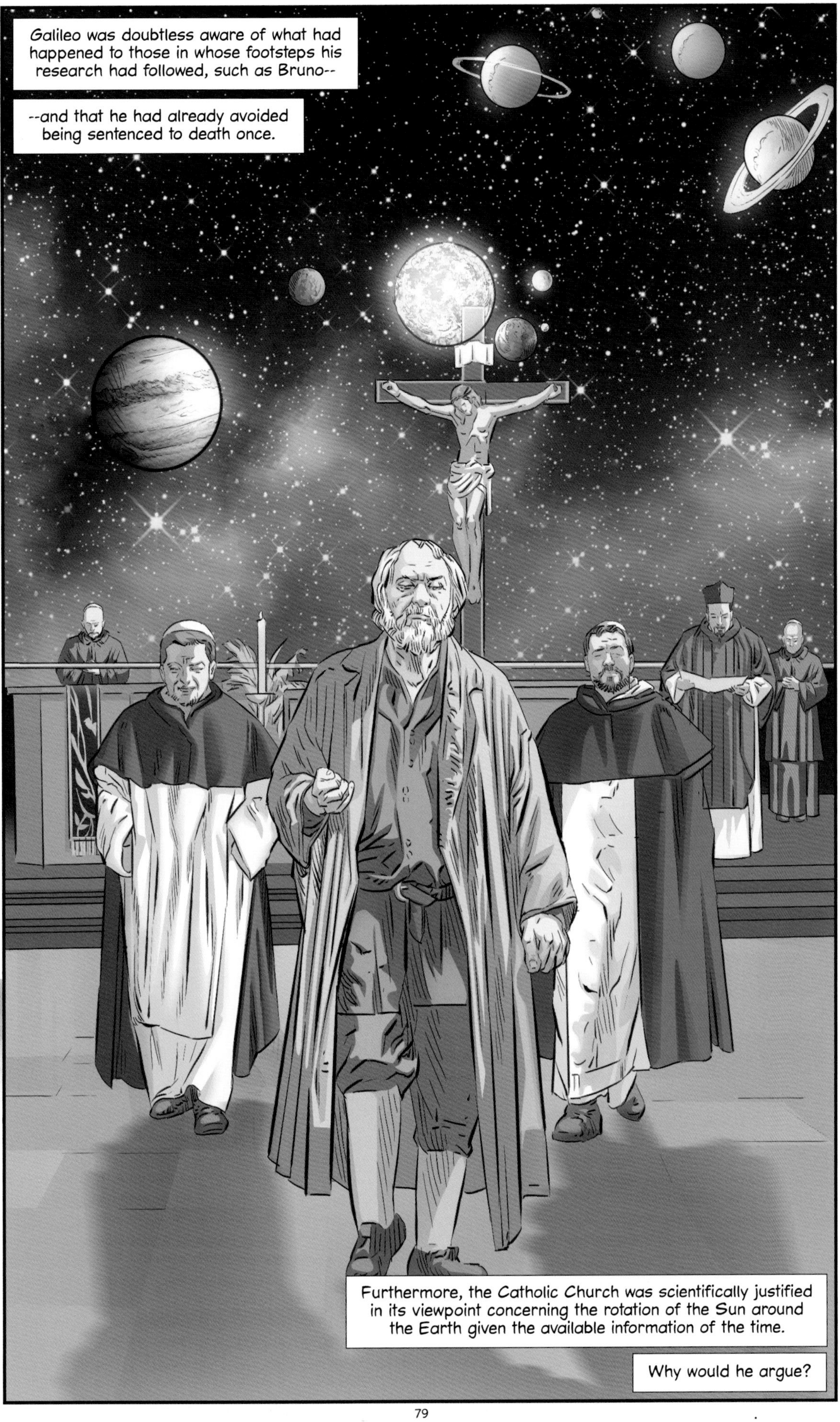
Galileo was doubtless aware of what had happened to those in whose footsteps his research had followed, such as Bruno--
--and that he had already avoided being sentenced to death once.
Furthermore, the Catholic Church was scientifically justified in its viewpoint concerning the rotation of the Sun around the Earth given the available information of the time.
Why would he argue?

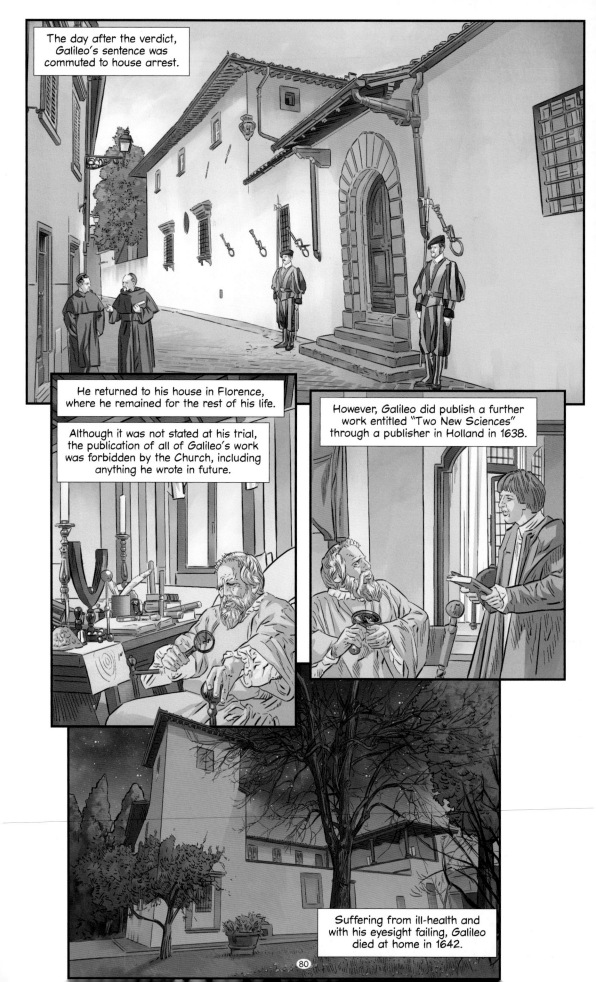

The day after the verdict, Galileo's sentence was commuted to house arrest.

He returned to his house in Florence, where he remained for the rest of his life.

Although it was not stated at his trial, the publication of all of Galileo's work was forbidden by the Church, including anything he wrote in future.

However, Galileo did publish a further work entitled "Two New Sciences" through a publisher in Holland in 1638.

Suffering from ill-health and with his eyesight failing, Galileo died at home in 1642.

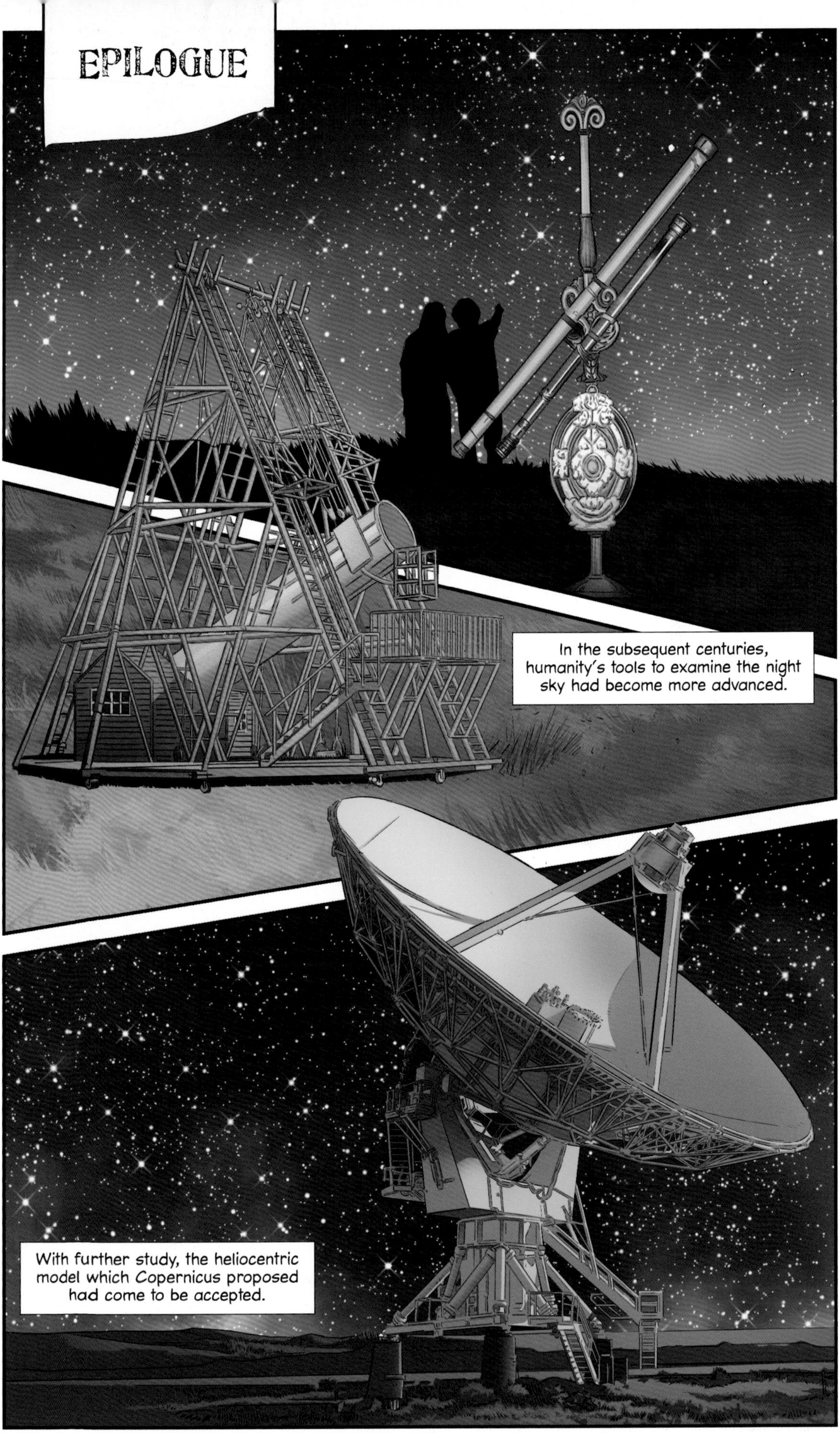
EPILOGUE
In the subsequent centuries, humanity's tools to examine the night sky had become more advanced.
With further study, the heliocentric model which Copernicus proposed had come to be accepted.

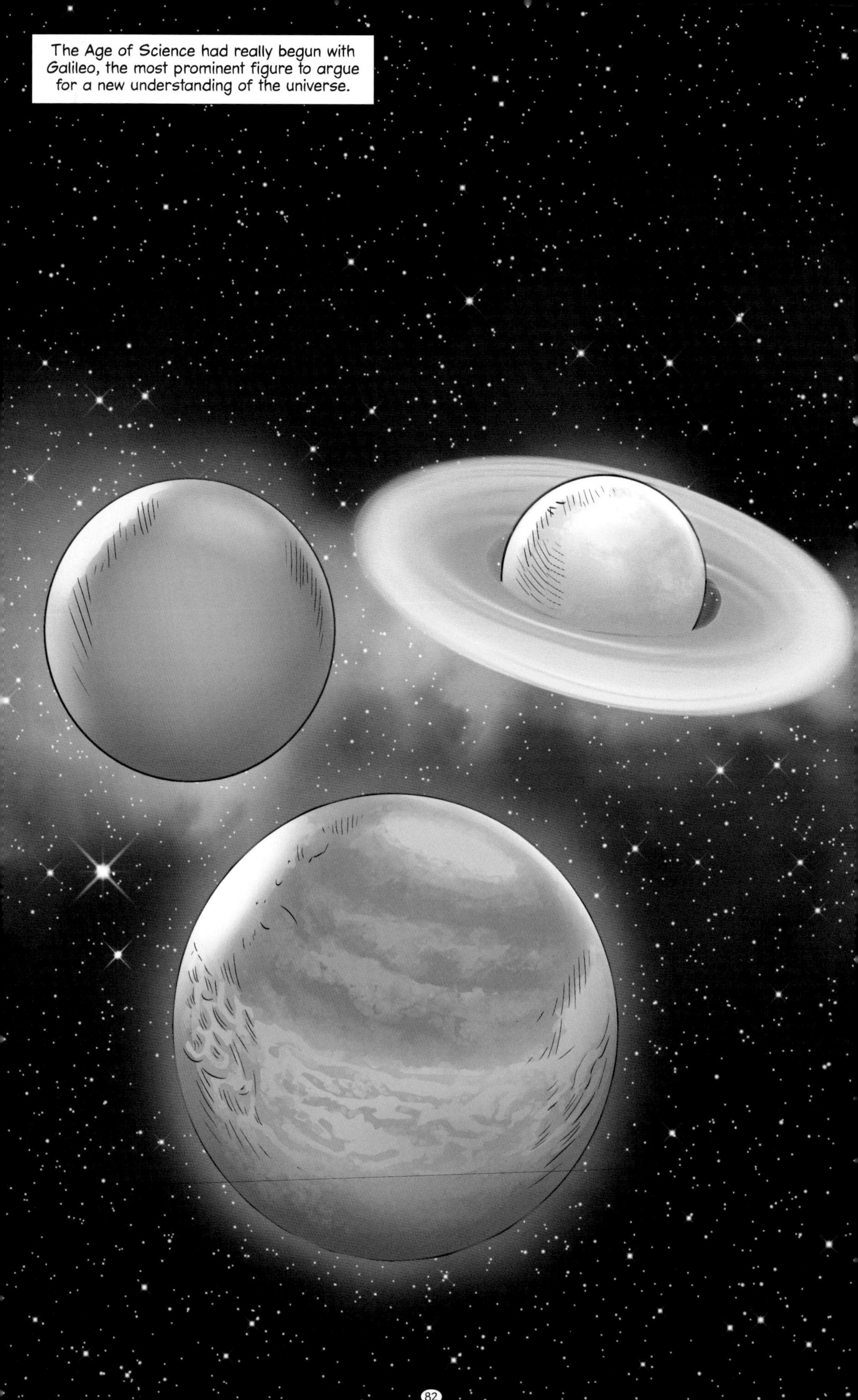
The Age of Science had really begun with Galileo, the most prominent figure to argue for a new understanding of the universe.

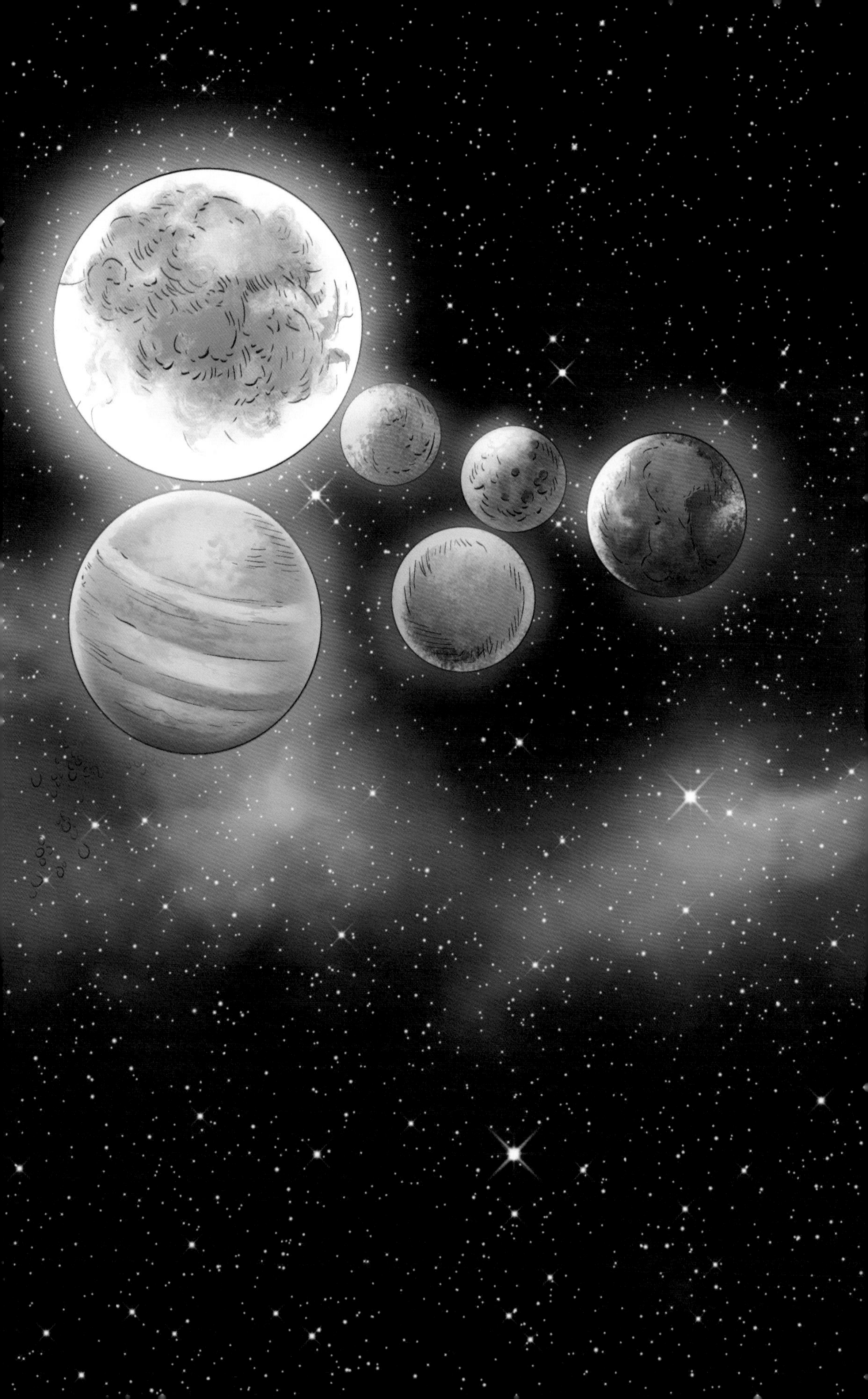

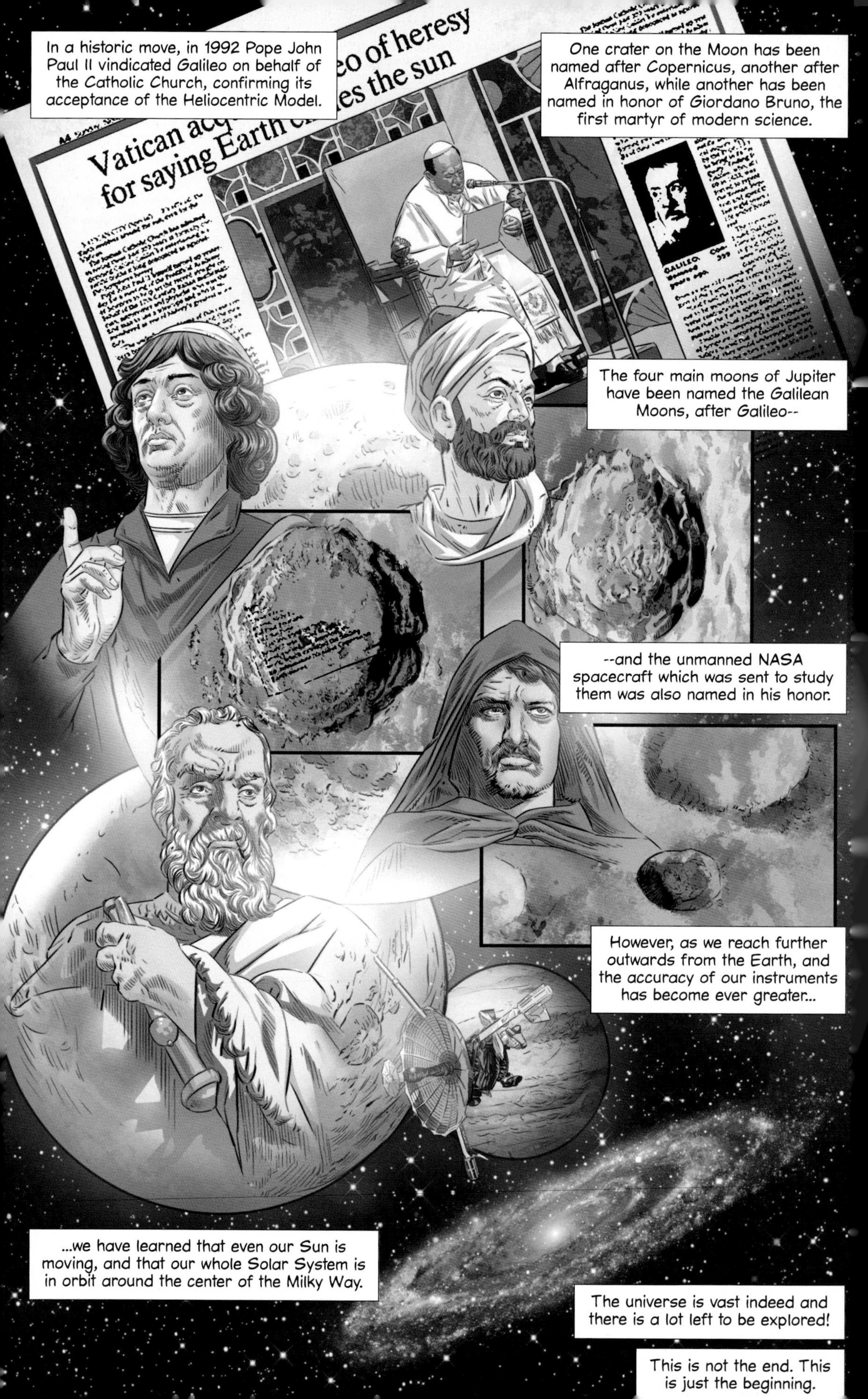
In a historic move, in 1992 Pope John Paul II vindicated Galileo on behalf of the Catholic Church, confirming its acceptance of the Heliocentric Model.
Vatican acq... ...eo of heresy for saying Earth ci...es the sun
One crater on the Moon has been named after Copernicus, another after Alfraganus, while another has been named in honor of Giordano Bruno, the first martyr of modern science.
The four main moons of Jupiter have been named the Galilean Moons, after Galileo--
--and the unmanned NASA spacecraft which was sent to study them was also named in his honor.
However, as we reach further outwards from the Earth, and the accuracy of our instruments has become ever greater...
...we have learned that even our Sun is moving, and that our whole Solar System is in orbit around the center of the Milky Way.
The universe is vast indeed and there is a lot left to be explored!
This is not the end. This is just the beginning.

ALSO IN THIS SERIES

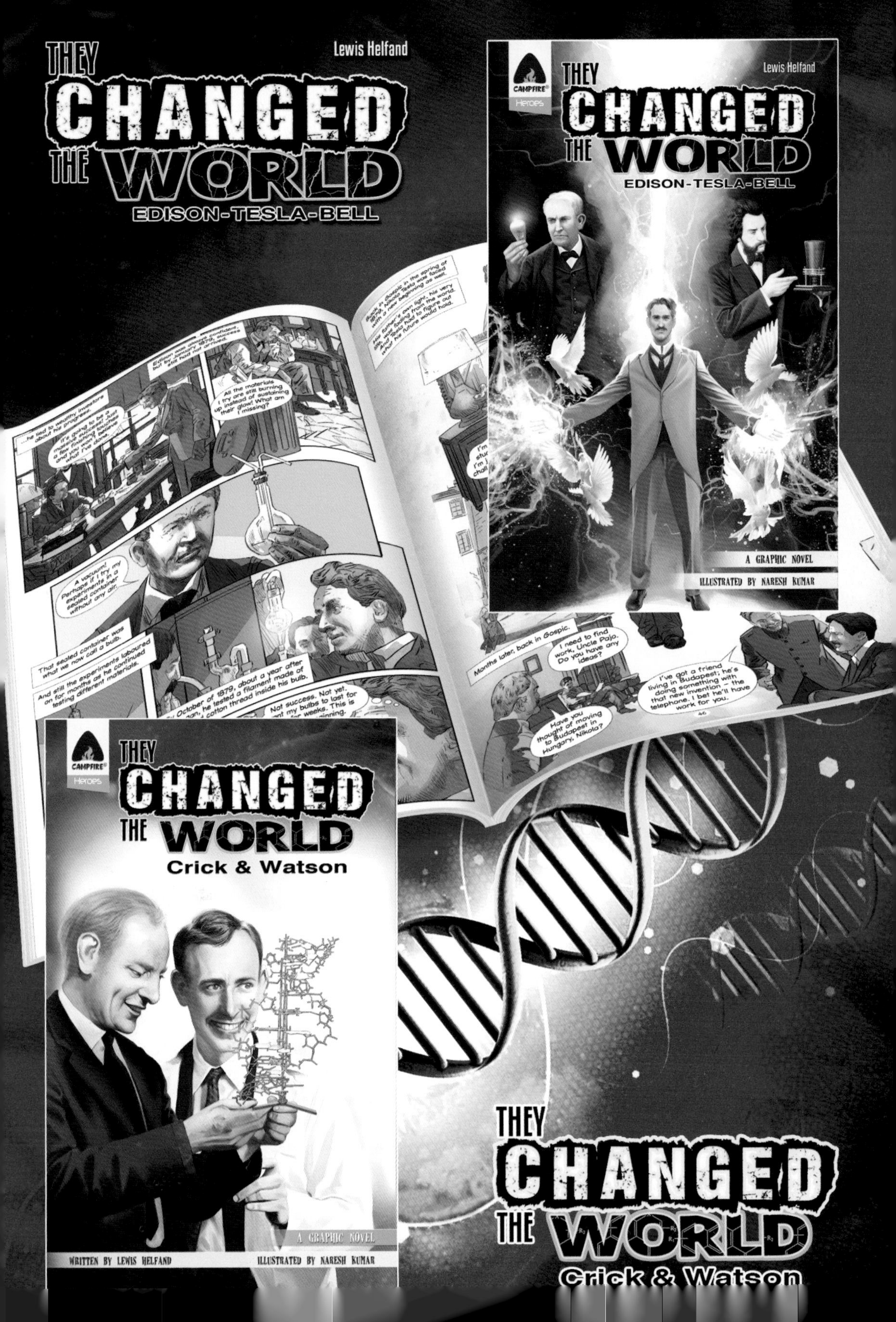
Lewis Helfand
THEY CHANGED THE WORLD
EDISON-TESLA-BELL
All the materials I try are still burning up instead of sustaining their glow! What am I missing?
A vacuum! Perhaps if I try my experiments in a sealed container without any air.
That sealed container was what we now call a bulb.
And still the experiments laboured on for months as he continued testing different materials.
Months later, back in Gospic.
I need to find work, Uncle Pajo. Do you have any ideas?
Have you thought of moving to Budapest in Hungary, Nikola?
I've got a friend living in Budapest; he's doing something with that new invention – the telephone. I bet he'll have work for you.
46
CAMPFIRE
Heroes
Lewis Helfand
THEY CHANGED THE WORLD
EDISON-TESLA-BELL
A GRAPHIC NOVEL
ILLUSTRATED BY NARESH KUMAR
CAMPFIRE
Heroes
THEY CHANGED THE WORLD
Crick & Watson
A GRAPHIC NOVEL
WRITTEN BY LEWIS HELFAND
ILLUSTRATED BY NARESH KUMAR
THEY CHANGED THE WORLD
Crick & Watson

THE ROLE OF ANCIENT INDIAN
ASTRONOMERS

In Indian languages, the science of astronomy is called Khagola-shastra. Khagola was the astronomical observatory at the University of Nalanda (in present day Bihar, India). It was here where Aryabhatta, the famous 5th century Indian Astronomer, studied and extended the subject.

Aryabhatta presented a mathematical system that showed that the Earth spins on its axis. He also made an accurate approximation of the Earth's circumference and diameter, and also discovered how the lunar eclipse and solar eclipse happened for the first time. He gave the radius of the planetary orbits in terms of the radius of the Earth/Sun orbit as essentially their periods of rotation around the Sun.

The lack of a telescope hindered further advancement of ancient Indian astronomy. Though it should be admitted that with their observations with ancient instruments, the astronomers in ancient India were able to arrive at near perfect measurement of astronomical movements and predict eclipses. Indian astronomers also propounded the theory that the Earth was a sphere.

Aryabhatta's magnum opus, the "Aryabhattiya" was translated into Latin in the 13th century. Through this translation, European mathematicians got to know methods for calculating the areas of triangles, volumes of spheres as well as square root and cube root. Aryabhatta's ideas about eclipses and the sun being the source of moonlight may not have caused much of an impression on European astronomers as by then they had come to know of these facts through the observations of Copernicus and Galileo.

Varahamihira, in 6th century, had claimed that there should be a force which might be keeping bodies stuck to the Earth, and also keeping heavenly bodies in their determined places. Thus, the concept of the existence of some kind of force that governs the falling of objects to the Earth and their staying there was recognized much before (although the heliocentric theory of gravitation was also developed in around 500 B.C. by Greek astronomers).

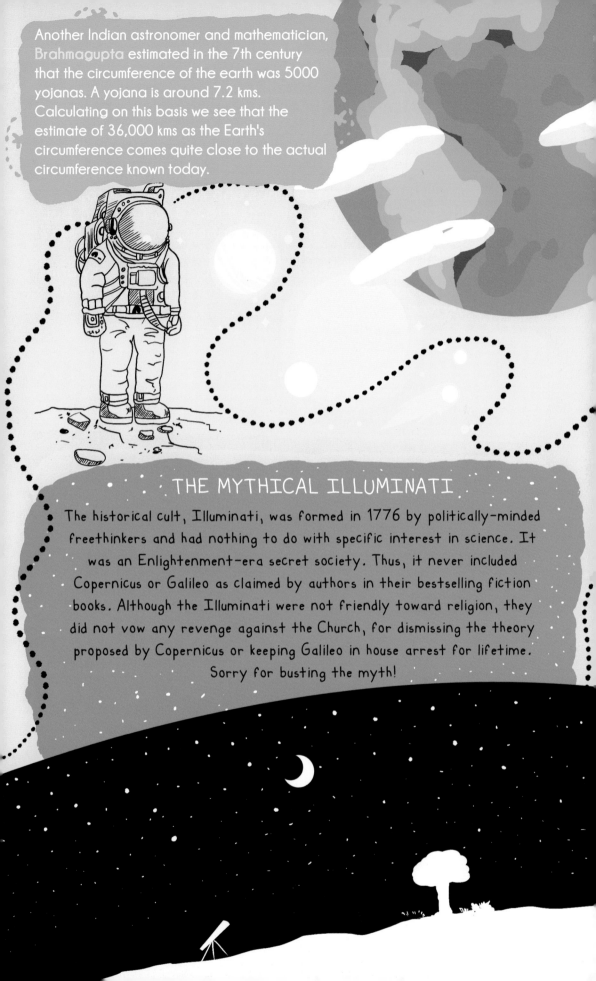

Another Indian astronomer and mathematician, Brahmagupta estimated in the 7th century that the circumference of the earth was 5000 yojanas. A yojana is around 7.2 kms. Calculating on this basis we see that the estimate of 36,000 kms as the Earth's circumference comes quite close to the actual circumference known today.

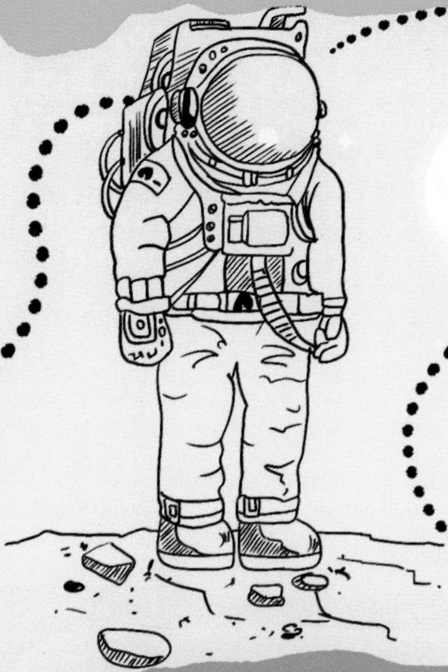

THE MYTHICAL ILLUMINATI

The historical cult, Illuminati, was formed in 1776 by politically-minded freethinkers and had nothing to do with specific interest in science. It was an Enlightenment-era secret society. Thus, it never included Copernicus or Galileo as claimed by authors in their bestselling fiction books. Although the Illuminati were not friendly toward religion, they did not vow any revenge against the Church, for dismissing the theory proposed by Copernicus or keeping Galileo in house arrest for lifetime. Sorry for busting the myth!

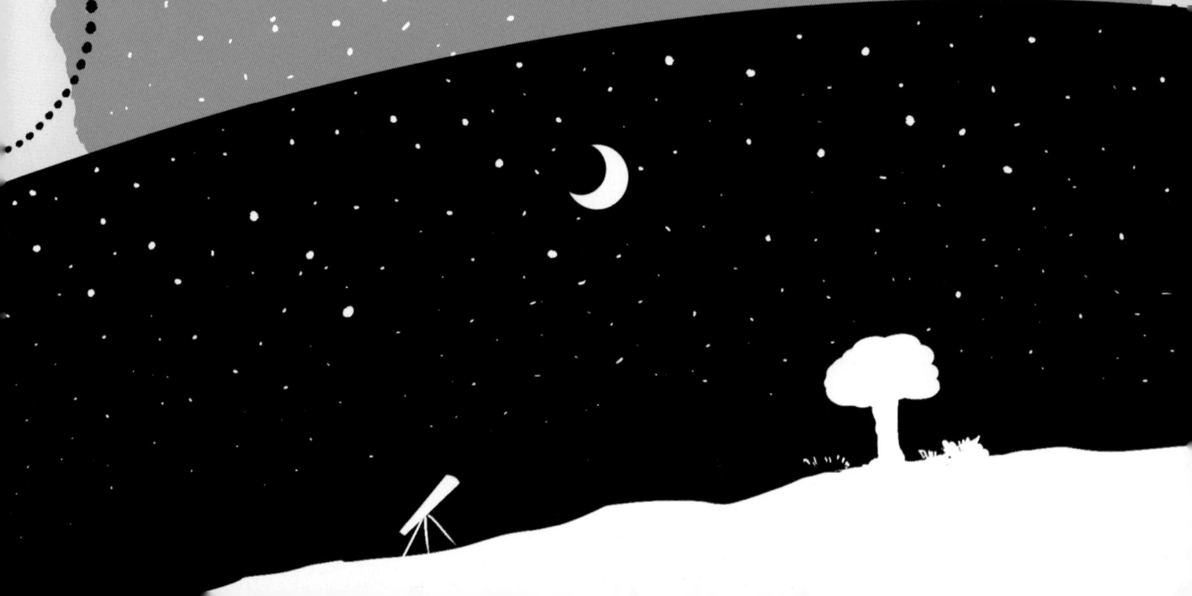

THE HOLY SIDE OF
THE PLANETS

Everyone knows the names of the planets—Mercury, Venus, Earth, Mars, Jupiter, Saturn, Uranus and Neptune (Pluto was a planet till 2006, when it was relegated to a dwarf planet). But has anyone wondered how did these planets get their names? Most of the planets were named after gods by the ancient civilizations, as these were the celestial objects in the sky and were usually referred to as "wandering stars". Even the word planet is derived from ancient Greek.

1. Mercury was named by the Romans after their most important god, the messenger god and the god of travellers. It was the fastest planet as it moved closest to the Sun.

2. Venus was named by the Romans after the goddess of love and beauty. They named it so as it was the brightest star in the sky after the Sun and the Moon. It was also referred to as the Morning star.

3. Earth is the only planet which is not named after a god or a goddess. The name is derived from Old English word which means ground.

4. Mars was named after the Roman god of war because of its red color.

5. Jupiter was named after the king of the Roman gods, as its the biggest planet in the system.

6. Saturn was named after the Roman god of agriculture. It was named so because of its golden color.

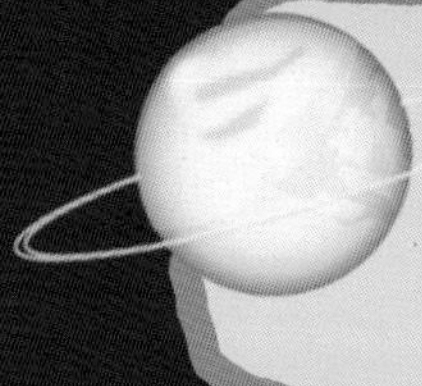

7. Uranus was named after Saturn's father in Roman mythology. Even though the planet was discovered in 1800s, the astronomers decided to carry on the tradition of naming planets after gods and goddesses.

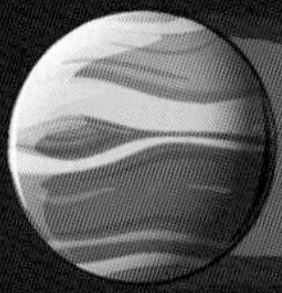

8. Neptune was named after the god of the sea, because of its blue color.

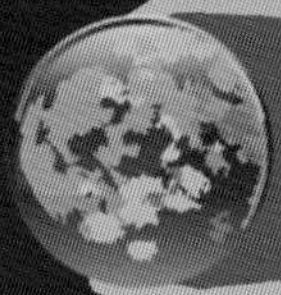

9. Pluto was named after the god of the underworld. It was also named after the scientist who predicted the planet's existence, Percival Lowell.

THROUGH THE LENS

- 3rd century BC – Greek mathematician Euclid first wrote scientific overview of sun rays, reflection and refraction. His work was expanded 5 centuries later by Ptolemy.
- 10-12th century – Several Arab scientists started examining the properties of light, mirrors, lenses and more. Ibn al-Haytham's "Book of Optics" arrives in Europe, and after translation to Latin, it becomes the foundation of modern European exploration of lenses.
- 1608 – German-Dutch spectacle-maker Hans Lippershey applies his patent on what is today known as telescope.
- 1609 – Famous astronomer, Galileo Galilei managed to improve the basic telescope design of Hans Lippershey, calling it "perspicillum".
- 1611 – The name "telescope" is coined by Greek mathematician Giovanni Demisiani for Galileo's instrument.
- 1611 – Johannes Kepler provided detailed scientific explanation about the inner workings of telescopes. He also created the first telescope that was focused only on astronomy.
- 1616 – 1684 – Large amount of scientific effort is focused on further development of telescopes by Christian Huygens, James Gregory, Isaac Newton, Laurent Cassegrain and Robert Hooke.
- 1897 – Yerkes Observatory builds the largest telescope of its time – 101.6cm refractor telescope.
- 1910 – One of the most famous telescope designs is created - Ritchey-Chrétien telescope by American astronomer George Willis Ritchey and French astronomer Henri Chrétien.
- 1970 – First telescope launched into space onboard probe, Uhuru. This was also the first gamma-ray telescope ever to be used.
- 1990 – Hubble telescope launched into Earth's orbit. It quickly became one of the most famous and most important telescopes ever to be built.
- 2009 – Kepler telescope launched in space, with goal of locating planets that are orbiting our neighboring stars. It has 2.4m diameter mirror.
- 2011 – NASA announces plans to launch the most ambitious space telescope of all time. James Webb Space Telescope will operate in deep space and have a staggering 6.5m diameter mirror. The work will be completed by 2020.

ISRO: 50 YEARS OF SPACE EXPLORATION
(Indian Space Research Organisation)

2001

GSLV (Geosynchronous Satellite Launch Vehicle) was launched.

2002

Kalpana-1 (satellite) was launched.

2008

India's Chandrayaan-1 first moon mission was launched by PSLV.

1993

PSLV (Polar Satellite Launch Vehicle) was developed in 1990s and has become the Indian space mission's most reliable workhorse. It launched several satellites for historic missions like Chandrayaan and Mangalyaan.

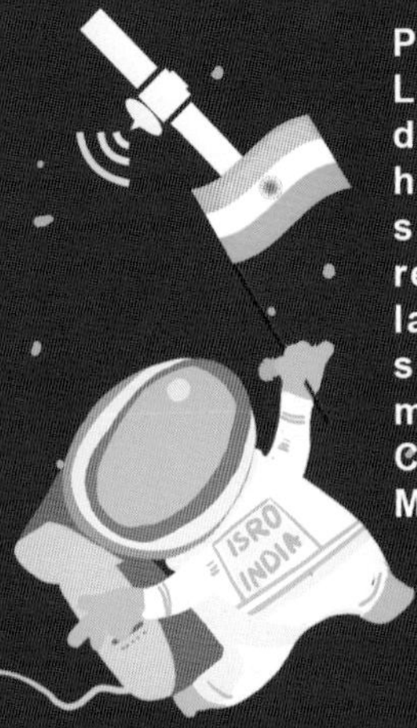
ISRO
INDIA

1984

A joint manned mission of India and Soviet Union was launched. In this mission the first Indian cosmonaut, Rakesh Sharma, spent eight days in Russian space station Salyut-7.

1969

Indian Space Research Organisation (ISRO) was formed.

1963

The first sounding rocket is launched from Thumba Equatorial Rocket Launching Station in Kerala. It marks the beginning of the Indian space program. Dr APJ Abdul Kalam was part of the team.

1968

Experimental Satellite Communication Earth Station set up in Ahmedabad, Gujarat.

1967

Satellite Telecommunication Earth Station set up at Ahmedabad, Gujarat on 1 January 1967.

1965

Space Science and Technology Centre (SSTC) was established in Thumba, Kerala on 1 January 1965.

1962

Dr Vikram Sarabhai and physicist Kalpathi Ramakrishna Ramanathan formed The Indian National Committee for Space Research.

2014

India's first interplanetary mission to the planet Mars known as Mars Orbiter mission (MOM) or Mangalyaan was launched. On 24 September, 2014, MOM entered Mars orbit. India became the first country in the world to insert a spacecraft into the Martian orbit in its very first attempt.

2019

On 15 July, 2019 Chandrayaan-2 Moon Mission was launched.

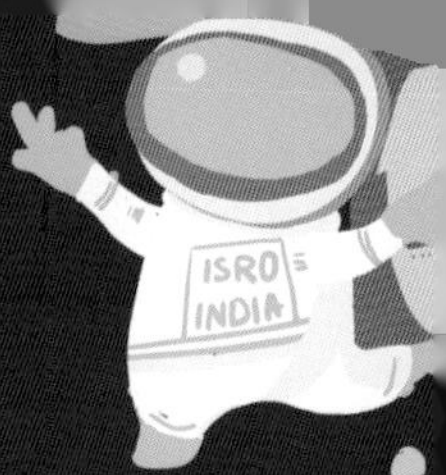
ISRO
INDIA

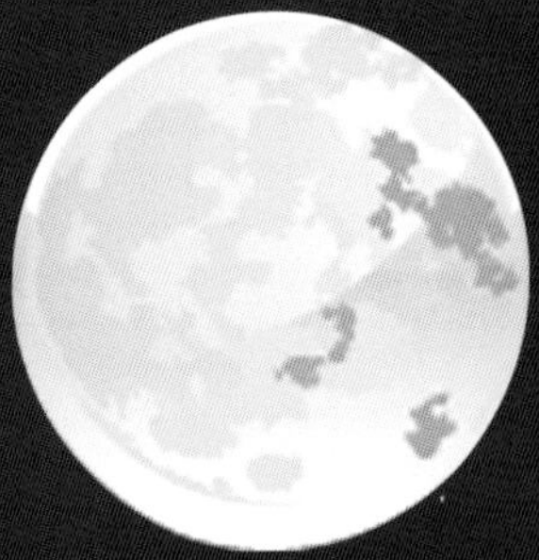

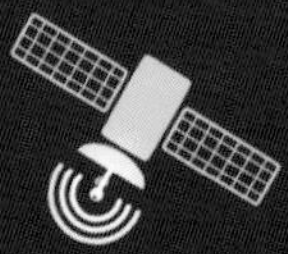

1981

Satellite Rohini was placed into orbit.

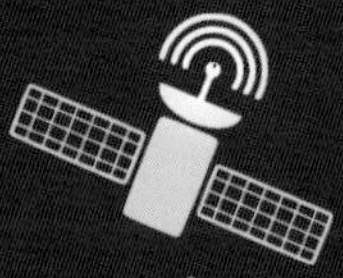

1980

India's first experimental satellite vehicle was launched-Satellite launch Vehicle-3 (SLV-3)-which made ISRO sixth nation in space program.

1979

The first experimental remote-sensing satellit Bhaskara-I, was built a launched in India.

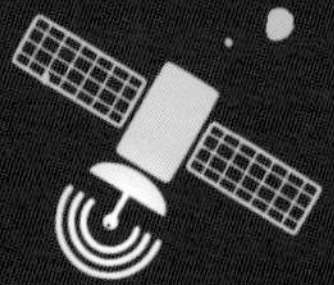

1971

Satish Dhawan Space Centre formed in Sriharikota, Andhra Pradesh. It is the site where most of the rockets will be launched from.

1972

Department of Space (DoS) established and ISRO brought under it.

1975

On 19 April, first Indian satellite, Aryabhata was launched into space. It marked a milestone in India's space programme.

SPACE: SEEKING NEW FRONTIERS

Humanity has come a long way since the pioneering insights provided by Copernicus, Bruno and Galileo. Today, deep space is not beyond us any longer. Inspired by the efforts of the NASA of the United States, and the Soviet Union in the 1950s, all nations today aspire to a viable space program, and many have succeeded. In addition to the United States and Russia, the European Union, Japan, China, India and many other nations have successful programs sending satellites into space.

India was a relatively early entrant in the space race, when in 1963, a Nike Apache sounding rocket was launched from the Thumba Equatorial Rocket Launching Station (TERLS). Today, the Indian space program is managed by the Indian Space Research Organisation (ISRO). ISRO has been successful in launching numerous satellites and has also sent orbiters to the Moon and Mars.

PIONEERING INDIAN ROCKETMEN

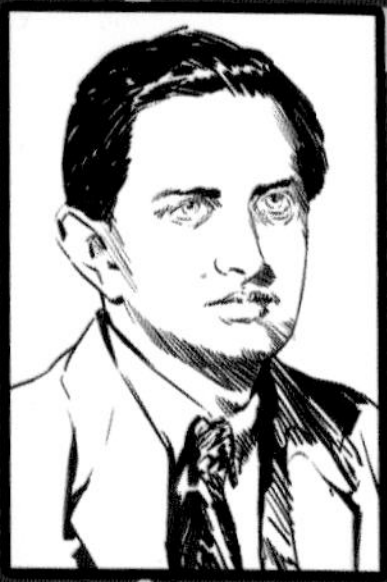

Dr VIKRAM SARABHAI

He started a project for the launch of an Indian satellite. Due to his efforts, in 1975, the satellite Aryabhata was successfully launched and put in orbit around the Earth. He is the founding father of Indian Space Research Organisation (ISRO) at Bengaluru, Karnataka.

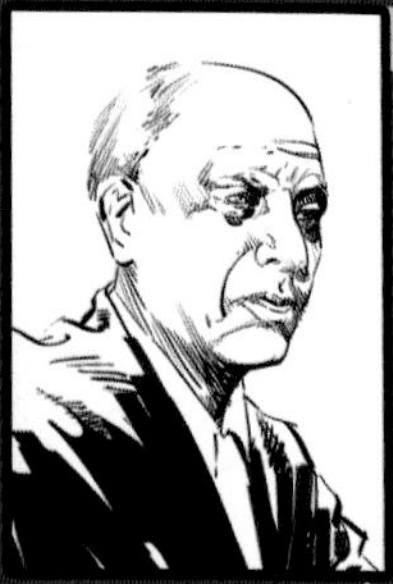

KALPATHI RAMAKRISHNAN RAMANATHAN

He was the Director of Physical Research Laboratory, Ahmedabad. He played a very important role in the early Indian space programme, by testing sounding rockets and helping to develop the Thumba Equatorial Rocket Launching Station (TERLS).

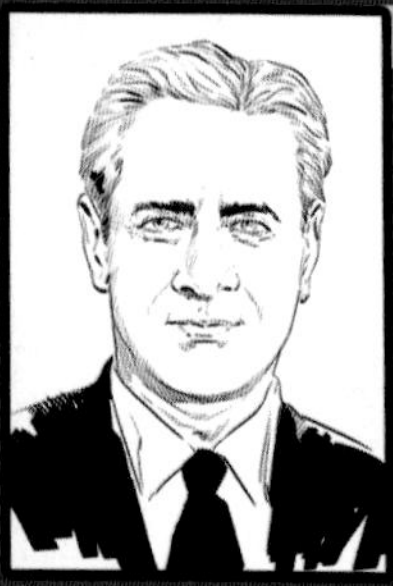

SATISH DHAWAN

He was the chairman of ISRO and is widely regarded as the father of experimental fluid dynamics research in India. He spearheaded many important projects like Indian Remote Sensing satellite (IRS) and Polar Satellite Launch Vehicle (PSLV). His efforts propelled India into the forefront of global space race.

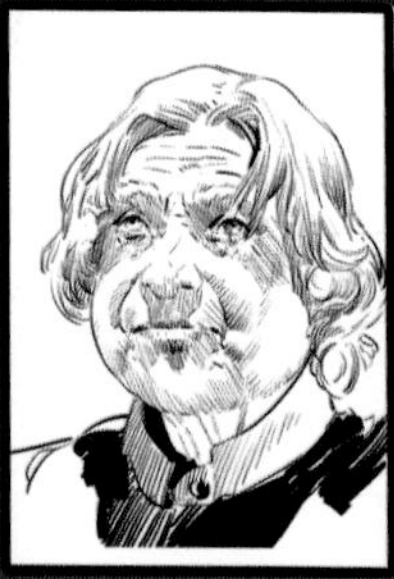

Dr APJ ABDUL KALAM

He was a project director at ISRO and the 11th President of India. He was closely involved with India's civilian space programme and military missile development efforts. Thus, he was also known as the "Missile Man of India".

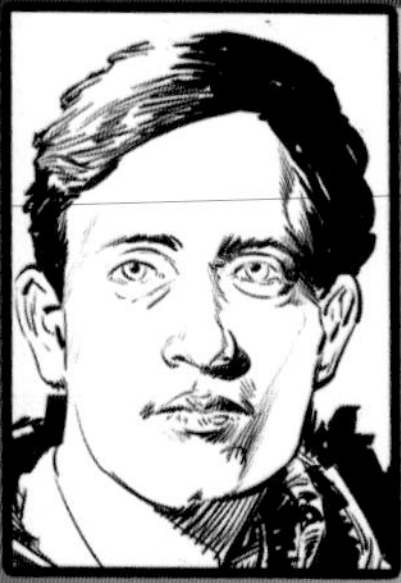

RAKESH SHARMA

He is the first and only Indian citizen to travel to space till date. It was a joint space venture between ISRO and Soviet Interkosmos in 1984, and Rakesh Sharma was one of the cosmonauts in Salyut-7.

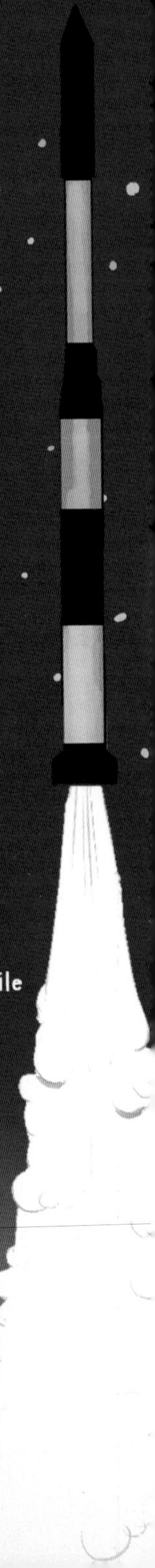

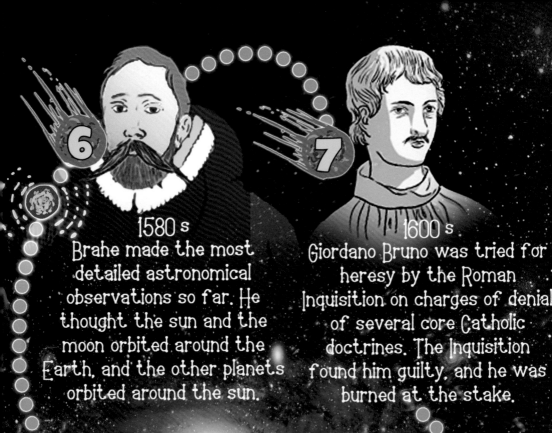

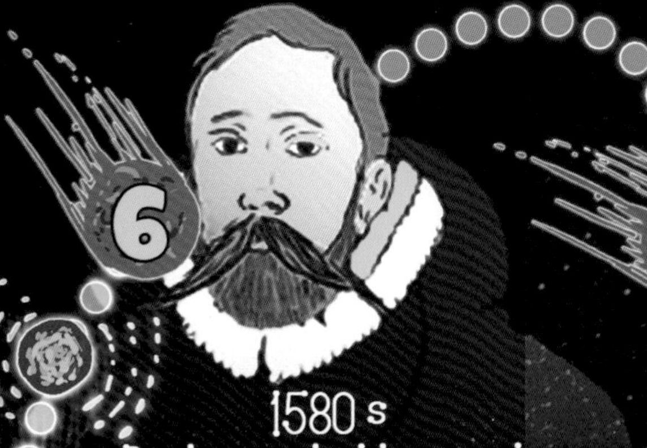
6

1580 s
Brahe made the most detailed astronomical observations so far. He thought the sun and the moon orbited around the Earth, and the other planets orbited around the sun.

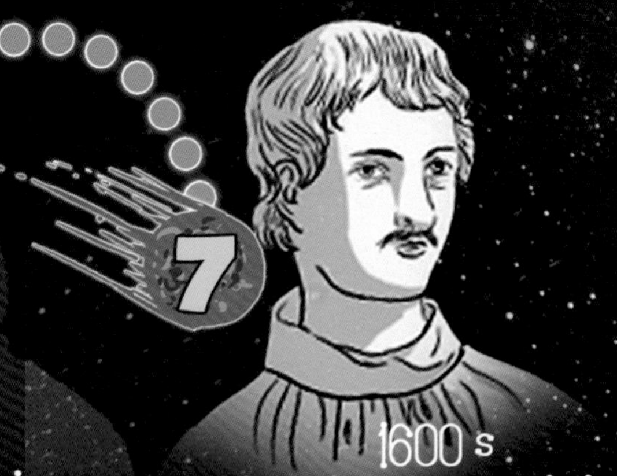
7

1600 s
Giordano Bruno was tried for heresy by the Roman Inquisition on charges of denial of several core Catholic doctrines. The Inquisition found him guilty, and he was burned at the stake.

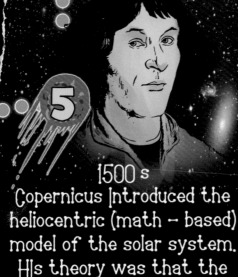

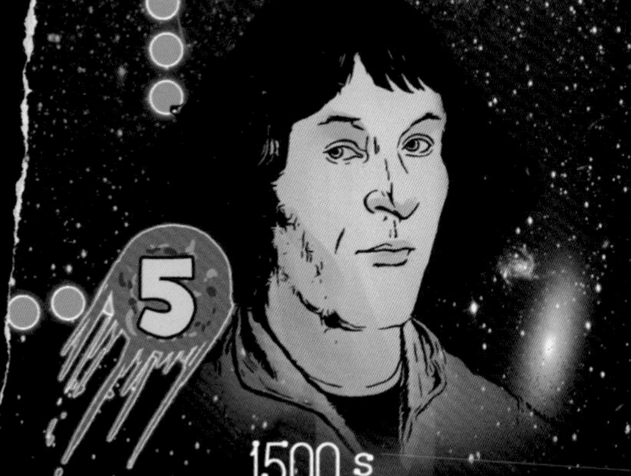
5

1500 s
Copernicus Introduced the heliocentric (math – based) model of the solar system. HIs theory was that the sun was the center of the universe and the planets revolved around the sun.

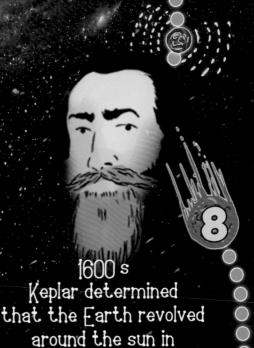

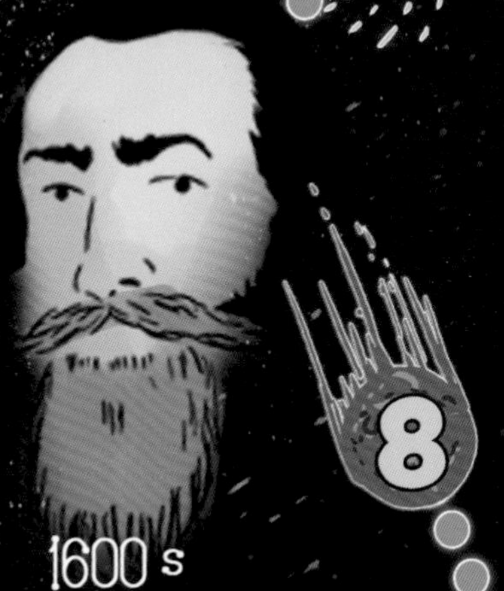
8

1600 s
Keplar determined that the Earth revolved around the sun in ellipses. Also developed three laws that described planetary motion.

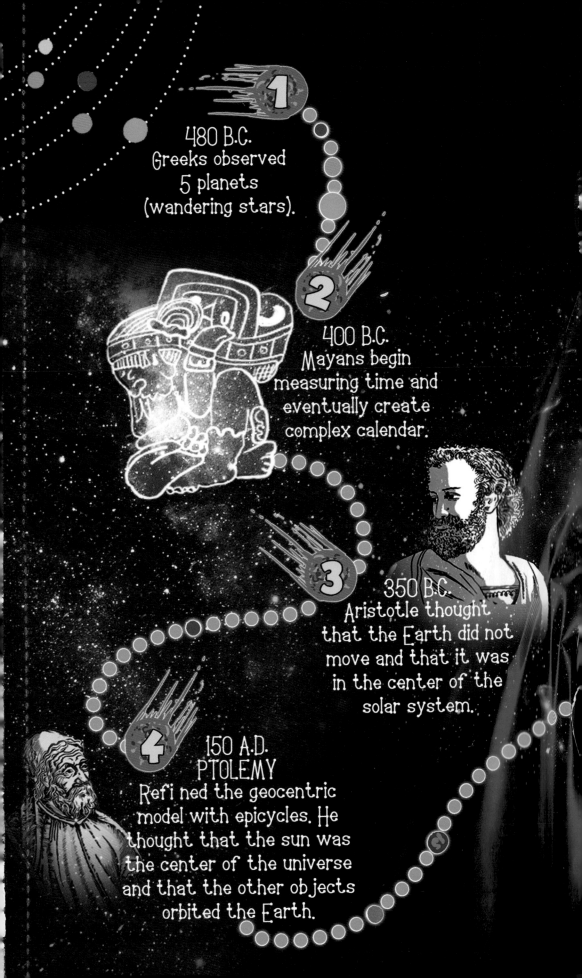

1

480 B.C.
Greeks observed 5 planets (wandering stars).

2

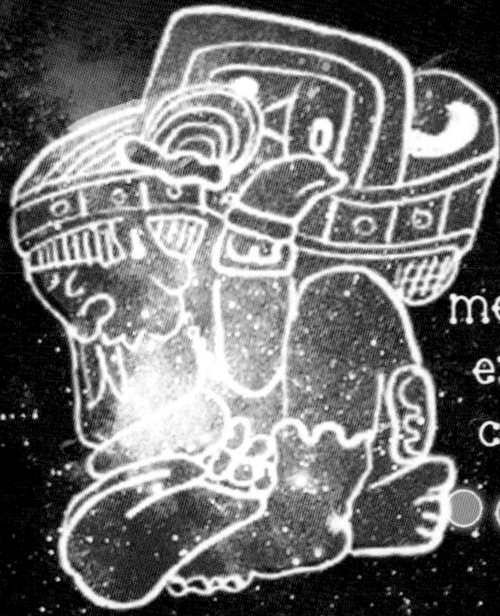

400 B.C.
Mayans begin measuring time and eventually create complex calendar.

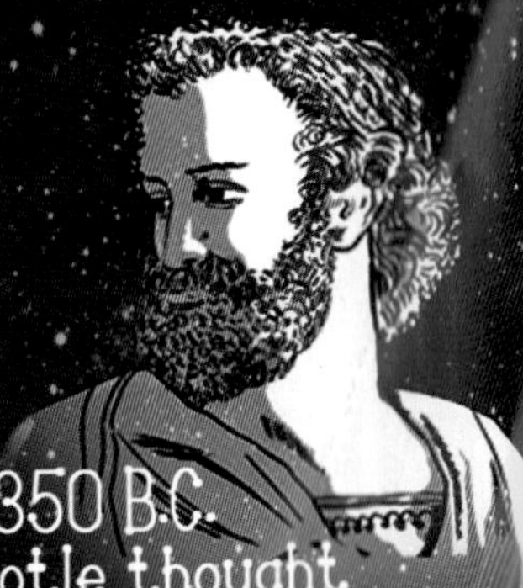

3

350 B.C.
Aristotle thought that the Earth did not move and that it was in the center of the solar system.

4

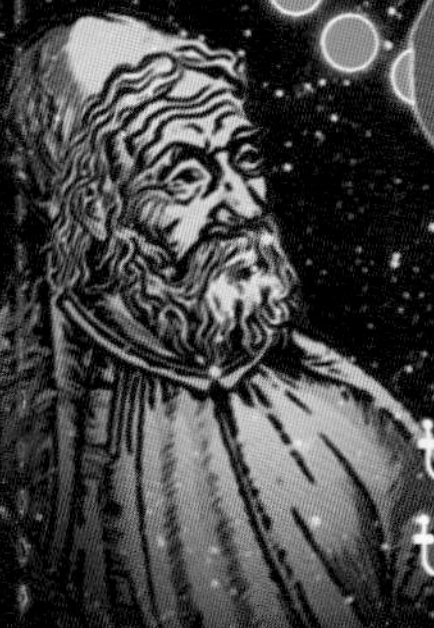

150 A.D.
PTOLEMY
Refi ned the geocentric model with epicycles. He thought that the sun was the center of the universe and that the other objects orbited the Earth.

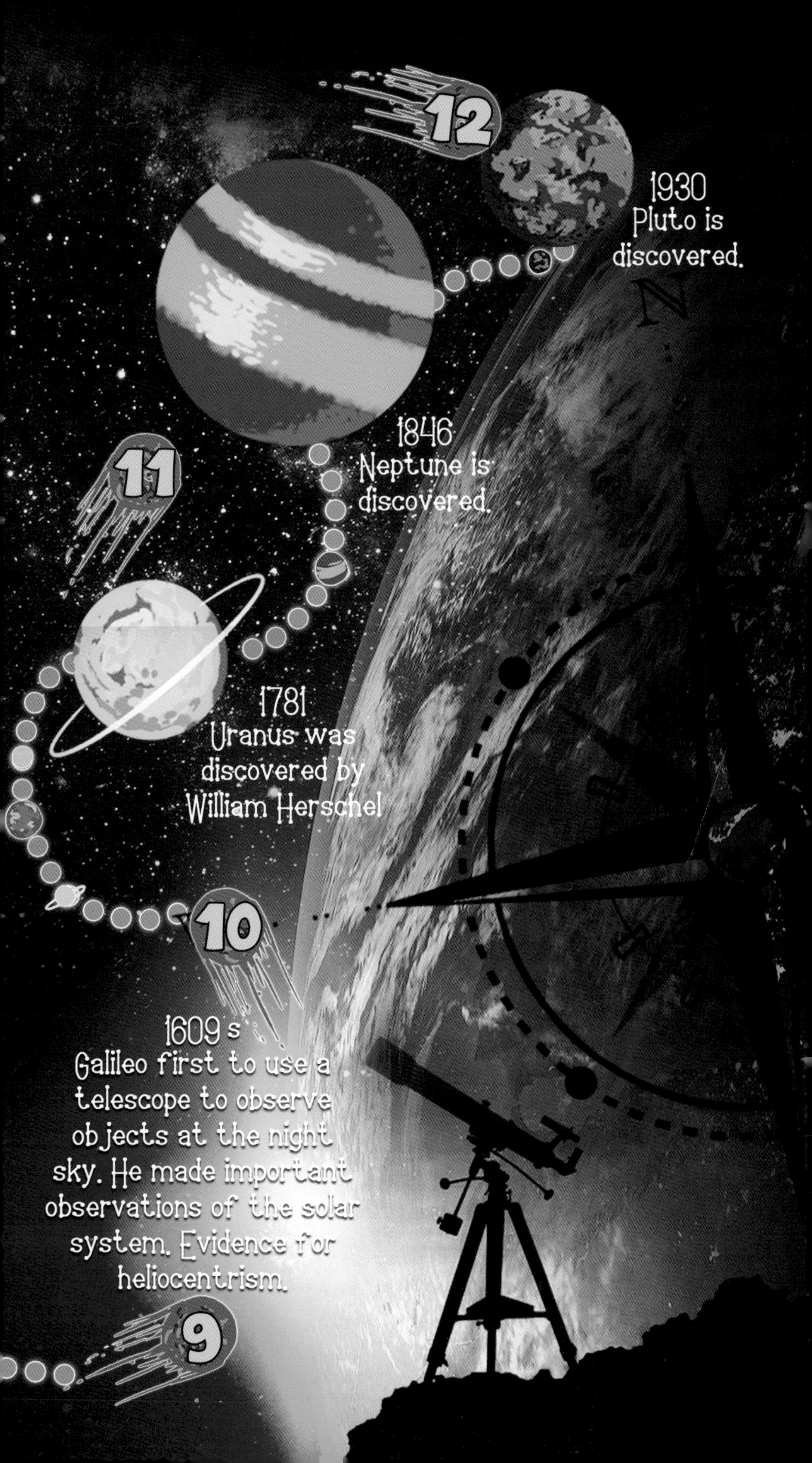
9
1609 s
Galileo first to use a telescope to observe objects at the night sky. He made important observations of the solar system. Evidence for heliocentrism.
10
1781
Uranus was discovered by William Herschel
11
1846
Neptune is discovered.
12
1930
Pluto is discovered.